WHEN THEY WON'T QUIT

A Call To Action for Families, Friends and Employers of Alcohol and Drug-Addicted People

WHEN THEY WON'T QUIT

A Call To Action for Families, Friends and Employers of Alcohol and Drug-Addicted People

BRUCE COTTER

Holly Hill Publishing
Hunt Valley, Maryland

Unattributed quotations are by Bruce Cotter

Library of Congress Cataloging-in-Publication Data
Control Number: 2002103932

Cotter, Bruce
When They Won't Quit: a call to action for families, friends and employers of alcohol and drug-addicted people

1. Helping those who don't want help with addiction. 2. Recognizing and understanding chemical dependency. 3. Intervention. 4. Treatment. 5. Long-term recovery.
Includes appendix
ISBN, print ed. 0-9719338-2-0

Published by:
Holly Hill Publishing
Post Office Box 309
Hunt Valley, Maryland 21030 U.S.A

Printed in the United States of America
First Edition

My heartfelt thanks to those
who extended their hands
to me long before
I could extend mine to them.

To my wife Suzanne,
the most magnificent woman I have ever known.
As is always the case, nothing happens without you.

All my love as ever and forever.

For Suzanne and Quinn,
the wind and the sails of my boat.

ACKNOWLEDGMENTS

Joe Quinn and David Shay did not help to write this book, they are this book. Any aspect of this book you find helpful, interesting or of value probably came from them. Any points you find particularly brilliant definitely came from them. While they are no longer with us, the echoes of their knowledge of addiction and treatment thankfully continue. I am grateful for the guidance and insight they gave me and I am blessed that I was once able to say that they were my very best friends.

Tom McDougal is one of the finest addiction counselors I have known. Thirteen years ago, he believed I could and would live sober. During a difficult twenty-eight day period in 1989, he convinced me of the same. Tom is a sensitive, learned and gentle man. This was apparent when I learned that he referred to me as the "sickest son-of-a #@$&! in the entire hospital"—and this was a big hospital. Tom said that with sobriety "every morning can be Christmas morning." He was right.

Chuck Parsons has been my friend since I was nine years old. Without even trying, perhaps without even knowing, he has been influential in so many aspects of my life. One of the country's great orthopedic surgeons turned brilliant artist, Chuck's greatest talent of all is knowing how to be a friend.

Locke Rush and Edwina Carr are valued friends who encouraged me to write this book. Two talented writers as well as leaders in the field of chemical dependence, they convinced me I might have something to contribute.

Greg Lawrence, with patience and kindness, endured my endless ramblings and kept me focused on the task at hand. With his extraordinary talents, he took our countless hours of conversations and sculpted them into the clear flowing pages I know you will appreciate. With his keen sense and feel for the recovery process, Greg enabled me to convey the messages I hope will prove helpful.

Bonnie Egan has been a receptive, creative and patient editor. She has also been a delight to work with.

Robert Aulicino brought his years of creativity and experience to the tasks of cover design and interior layout. His knowledge and reassuring approach have been much needed, appreciated and respected.

CONTENTS

INTRODUCTION

HELPING THOSE WHO DON'T WANT HELP

If you are reading this book, chances are someone in your life has a problem with alcohol or drug abuse. You may not yet be sure how serious the problem is, but you are looking for help and guidance. You want to know what you can do today—what actions you can take to deal with the situation right now—because there is growing reason for concern and most likely his or her problem is causing problems for you as well.

The person is someone you care about—a husband or wife, a parent, a child or some other family member, an employee or co-worker, a friend or neighbor. Maybe you have noticed some erratic behavior, personality changes or signs of physical impairment. When questioned, the person may deny that any problem exists or may even blame you for causing the problem. He or she may have lied to you, broken promises or made excuses to try to justify behavior related to alcohol or drugs. Perhaps the person has been arrested or hospitalized or put into detox. The problem may involve excessive drinking or abuse of drugs such as marijuana, cocaine, heroin, amphetamines, barbiturates, prescription drugs, inhalants and so forth. Whatever the case may be, the important thing is that you are now looking for help. And help is readily available, even if the person doesn't want to be helped by you or by anybody else.

As a recovering alcoholic, I know from experience what the victims of drinking and drug abuse are going through.

Because all chemically dependent persons, to some extent, have lost touch with reality, they are almost always unable to help themselves. I have been a professional interventionist since 1990, working with people who have a problem with alcohol or other drugs—people who need help but don't want it. Clients come to me from every possible location, every walk of life and every age group. Many are educated professionals—bankers, lawyers, physicians, CEO's, airline pilots, clergy, entertainers, athletes. They are referred to me by treatment centers, employers, family doctors, churches and by people I've counseled or worked with in the past. I travel around the country and sometimes around the world to work with those in need. Always there is someone in the picture like you who cares enough to try to help.

Experience has taught me over and over that no matter how lost, hurt or despairing a person may be, it does not have to be that way. Nor does a chemically dependent person have to "hit bottom" before help can be accepted and initiated. The earlier you take action the more likely it will be that the person can fully recover. Those under the influence are usually in agony, though they may try to hide their condition. Sooner or later their pain will affect everyone around them. Why allow the situation to further deteriorate? Why prolong the suffering? I advise my clients to "decide to decide"—to make the decision to help now, not later when it may be too late. Why wait for some life-threatening crisis to occur? Why delay until the person destroys a marriage or loses a job, or God forbid, kills someone in an accident? Why hesitate when a life is on the line?

Make no mistake—all alcohol and substance abuse problems are *potentially fatal*. Chemical dependency is a progressive, chronic disease. We know with certainty that in most cases unless a chemically dependent person gets help, he or she will die prematurely. The causes of death, directly or indirectly linked to alcohol or drugs, are familiar to all of us: liver and heart diseases, automobile and on-the-job accidents, overdoses and suicides. The good news is that the disease is *treatable*; tragedies can be avoided by taking early, preemptive action to get the person into treatment. Through a well-established procedure known as "intervention," many thousands in recent decades have been able to reclaim their lives.

To intervene with a chemically dependent person means coming between the person and his or her drug of choice in order to instigate a course of treatment and to ultimately recover. Intervention is the first step that can be taken by people like you who care about the person with the problem. Ideally, it is a constructive, caring confrontation carried out as an act of compassion, with dignity and respect for all involved. The goal is not to punish, but to motivate the person to accept help for his or her illness. Because resistance to accepting treatment can be contentious, interventions require some form of professional guidance. An experienced interventionist can provide essential counseling and effectively intercede on behalf of family members to avoid antagonistic confrontations. I have acted in this confidential, loving capacity hundreds of times and can assure you that it works, relieving the emotional burden for those concerned and, over time, allowing wounds to heal.

The purpose of this book is to prepare you to decide on a course of action that is right for you and the person in your life who needs help. The first part, "Recognizing and Understanding Chemical Dependency," will enable you to identify the problem as an illness and to understand how it affects its victims. The second part of the book, "Intervention, Treatment and Long-term Recovery," will lead you step-by-step through the process of intervention, clinical treatment and continuing care.

The person you help today—especially when a family member is involved—will need your support during each phase of his or her recovery, and you may discover along the way that you, too, need to reach out for help. As described in the pages ahead, there are many options and resources available to you, including the Twelve Step programs such as Alcoholics Anonymous (AA) and Al-Anon. The journey to recovery may not be as easy or as straightforward as reading a book, but it can and should be a rewarding, life-fulfilling experience. It's not a penance—it's a blessing to be cherished and lived to the fullest. People can and do recover from chemical dependency, and so can the person in your life if you act in time.*

* In this book, the words "chemical dependency," "alcoholism," and "addiction," are used synonymously. While the drug of choice may be alcohol, heroin, cocaine, marijuana, prescription drugs or inhalants, the destructive condition caused by all mood-altering drugs is essentially the same regardless of the particular chemical or combination of substances involved. Moreover, the same remedial course of intervention and treatment is appropriate in each case.

PART ONE

RECOGNIZING AND UNDERSTANDING CHEMICAL DEPENDENCY

CHAPTER ONE

WHAT WE KNOW ABOUT CHEMICAL DEPENDENCY

THE DISEASE OF ALCOHOLISM

As the alcoholic son of an alcoholic mother, I've been dealing with the problem of chemical dependency for more than fifty years. But until I underwent clinical treatment in 1989, after surviving twenty years of my own drinking, I was unaware that alcoholism is a disease. In fact, the American Medical Association first classified alcoholism as a disease as early as 1956. Before that time, problem drinking was widely thought to be a symptom of some other underlying mental or emotional disorder. Now we know that addiction in all its forms is a *primary* disease that frequently causes or complicates other psychological and physical conditions.

As a first step to understanding and coming to grips with the problem, it is crucial for you to accept the fact that the person abusing alcohol or drugs is indeed suffering from an illness. Recognizing the disease for what it is will enable you, over time, to allay or set aside your feelings of anger, resentment and frustration. Such feelings are a natural consequence of the hurt and pain that we alcoholics inflict on others, especially on those who love us. But any animosity that you feel at this point, however justified, will only aggravate the situation and undermine your efforts to help. You may need to take a careful look inside yourself each step of the way to be sure that your motivation is to provide assistance and not to punish or to take retribution.

No one ever decides to become an alcoholic or drug

addict, just as no one decides to be stricken with cancer or any other potentially fatal disease. Our behavior as alcoholics is not deliberate—once the disease takes hold, we have little or no willful control over our actions. Chemical dependency is an involuntary, disabling condition. There is no point in blaming an alcoholic for being sick anymore than you would blame a child for coming down with a case of measles or chicken pox. The only reasonable response is to help the person get the care that he or she needs.

Medical experts remain divided over the ultimate cause of the disease, but most likely a combination of hereditary, environmental and psychological factors is involved. Over the years, a number of theories have been put forward to suggest there is a genetic predisposition to addiction. Alcoholism does tend to run in families—the chances are about one in four that a child of an alcoholic parent or parents will become an alcoholic. Yet for the majority of the more than twenty million alcoholics in this country, there is no family history of the disease. Nor is there a particular personality type associated with alcoholism. Some people appear to be vulnerable while others are not. The disease strikes indiscriminately, regardless of age, sex, ethnicity, education or occupation. None of these factors allows us to predict who will be afflicted.

Even without being able to fully explain how it is contracted, we can accurately diagnose the disease and describe in detail how it affects a wide population. What we know with certainty is that chemical dependency is not caused by any inherent weakness of character or lack of willpower. Nor does the disease manifest itself because of outside influences. We don't become alcoholics because of personal tragedies, failing marriages, difficulties on the job, mental stress or peer pressure. Contrary to what many alcoholics say, no one ever drives us to drink or use. We are driven by our own inner compulsion. In this regard, it is vitally important to understand that you are not the cause of someone you know having the disease. Whatever that person may say to the contrary, you are not at fault and there is no reason to blame yourself.

THE MASKS OF DENIAL

We alcoholics are experts at telling lies to hide the problem. There's an old saying about alcoholics that applies to other drug abusers as well—you can tell when they're lying because their lips are moving. But we're often not even aware that we're lying because we've lied to ourselves for so long that we've come to believe our own lies. We live in a world of ironclad delusions. That is why the chemically dependent person is almost never able to self-diagnose his or her condition. We can be sitting in a jail cell and still be able to deny reality. We don't connect our drinking and using with the crises that disrupt our lives, even run-ins with the law.

I know this only too well because it happened to me. I was once arrested for several outstanding bench warrants, all related to my past drinking. I found myself waiting in a cell and didn't know when I would get out—three days, thirty days, ninety days. No one told me. This actually occurred some months after I was sober, which was a further source of torment, because I thought that I was doing well at the time, having gone to dozens of AA meetings. But that was how it was back then. I never thought that if I didn't drink, I wouldn't be here now. It never occurred to me, even at that point when I should have known better.

Denial often takes the form of blaming others.

CASE NOTES: MONEY PROBLEMS?

I intervened with a woman executive who always seemed to have money problems. One time she said that she had been robbed at gunpoint and molested in a parking lot just after she returned from the bank to cash her paycheck. Her tirade against the security personnel and the police had everyone frightened. She threatened to have security people fired. Later, she privately confided to me that she had cashed her check and spent it on drugs.

Chemically dependent persons have no idea most of time what their real problem is. There may be periods of semi-awareness, like the morning after when we are looking in the mirror and gagging. In the throes of a hangover, we might even admit to ourselves, "I drank too much last night." We will resolve to cut back and promise our loved ones sincerely, "Never again," mistakenly believing that we can control our consumption and manage our lives. That is why people like you who are close to the addict are so important, because only you can identify the problem.

CASE NOTES: THE DRUNK TANK

One fellow I worked with was a top reporter with one of the country's leading newspapers. He had a severe alcohol problem and was prone to disappear for days at a time. On one occasion when he was missing for several days, his editor at the newspaper set about combing the city by phone, jail by jail, to locate him. Finally, the reporter was found in a "drunk tank" at one of the outlying precincts. The desk sergeant brought

the reporter in handcuffs to the phone and he nonchalantly asked his boss, "Hello, old buddy, what can I do
for you?" He had no idea that anything was wrong.

It may be difficult at first for you to see through our
efforts to conceal. Alcoholism is sometimes called the
"malaise of the gifted." However intelligent or talented any of
us may be, we are all astonishingly clever at hiding our problem. This defense manifests itself almost from the onset of our
illness. We live in constant dread that someone will find us
out. We will hide how much we earn and how much we owe;
we will hide where we live and whether or not we're married;
we will hide our education, our jobs, how tall we are, even our
names. We will go to the greatest lengths to hide how much we
are drinking and using. We hate questions. Our rule is *Don't
ask us anything* whether you are a spouse, a parent, a friend,
an employer, a doctor or a police officer. The only question
that we will tolerate is "What'll you have?"

When someone does happen to question us about our
drinking habits, our response will usually be some form of
denial. Any accusation or insinuation is likely to meet with
defensiveness, annoyance or outright hostility, even when
well-meaning concern prompts you to ask, "Don't you think
you might be drinking too much?" As sick as we are, we can
put on an impressive show of self-righteous indignation, and
we can be quite persuasive with our denials. At times we may
sound reasonable and sincere, especially during periods when
we are sober. We will insist that we are in complete control,
that it is our decision whether or not to drink, that we can quit
anytime we choose. But we never do, until someone like you
sees through our charade.

Depending on the social situation, we drinkers and users

have a variety of masks that we wear to deceive and manipulate those around us. It's as if we have a giant cabinet containing all of the comic and tragic faces that we present to the world. We have faces that we put on for the spouse, for the children, for the boss, for the priest or rabbi, for the therapist, and so on. Each person is treated to a different presentation. Our only purpose is to keep everyone tripping over themselves so we can continue using and abusing. This self-defeating game can go on for years.

THE CLINICAL NATURE OF ADDICTION

Alcoholism is a *progressive* disease, which means that if left untreated, it inevitably worsens over time. There may be periods of months and even years during which the person seems to improve, but sooner or later the downslide will continue and the disease will take its toll. Although the speed of its progression can vary from person to person, there are predictable stages leading up to premature death as the endpoint. Chemically dependent persons have an actuarial life expectancy that is at least ten years shorter than non-alcoholics. Late-stage alcoholics are typically diagnosed with physical ailments like cirrhosis of the liver, alcohol or drug-related heart disease, gastritis, ulcers, hepatitis, pancreatitis, brain seizures, strokes, deterioration of the lining of the esophagus, menstrual abnormalities in women, sexual impotence in men, various cancers, malnutrition, muscular atrophy and other physical maladies.

In addition, there are social and psychological problems that exacerbate over time. In my case, two marriages and a successful career in broadcasting were lost along the way, as were many friendships and countless opportunities in life. Depression and self-loathing eventually drove me to the brink of suicide. At this point, my self-loathing was so great, I felt I had forfeited my right to pray. How could God be interested in a bum like me? I went as far on one occasion as to put the barrel of a gun to my head, only to be distracted by my beloved golden retriever before I could bring myself to pull the trigger. Such extremes are not uncommon with alcoholics. If we don't take our lives by destroying our health physically or emotionally, we can do it accidentally behind the wheel of a car or through some other form of reckless behavior.

What the beer and wine commercials don't tell us is that alcohol is a depressant, a mood-altering drug that affects our brain chemistry and every facet of our existence. We are, for the most part, a tolerant society when it comes to drinking and using. Consumption of alcohol is legal and socially acceptable, while both prescription and illicit drugs readily lend themselves to widespread abuse. Our cultural attitudes make the problem of denial even more difficult to address. The line that separates the social drinker from the alcoholic can be confused in ways that disguise the illness. So-called casual or recreational drug use has been glamorized at times in the media, thus obscuring or minimizing the actual dangers of substance abuse. On the other hand, there is growing recognition by the courts and experts in the field that treatment rather than punishment is the more humane and cost-effective approach to the problem of alcohol and drug-related crime.

The disease is *chronic*, which means that it is a permanent, lifelong condition. As long as the alcoholic continues to drink or use, the disease will progress and the person's condition will deteriorate. There is no cure for chemical dependency, but it can be successfully treated and progression of the disease can be arrested in much the same way that some cancers are put into remission. Total abstinence from alcohol and all other mood-altering drugs will halt the alcoholic's downward spiral and effectively prevent the disease from running its deadly course.

THE TERMS OF RECOVERY

Sobriety requires a lifelong commitment because the illness will never go away—the non-drinking, non-using alcoholic will always be an alcoholic. This is why many who undergo treatment refer to themselves afterwards as "recovering" or "in recovery." They have come to realize that they will always be vulnerable to relapse. Even a taste of alcohol or a single episode with some other drug can put them back on the path to self-destruction. When it comes to these substances, they are simply incapable of moderation. There are alcoholics who stay sober for years only to return to drinking and using because they mistakenly think that they are no longer vulnerable, that time has somehow made them immune.

Relapses have been known to happen inadvertently when an injury or crisis leads a physician to prescribe a painkiller or tranquilizer. Even nonprescription cold remedies that contain alcohol can jeopardize the recovering alcoholic's sobriety. Because alcoholics and drug users commonly do not tell their doctors about their chemical dependencies, their doctors and/or therapists may fail to appreciate the fact that alcoholism is the primary, underlying disease that needs to be addressed before other emotional disorders such as depression and anxiety can be properly diagnosed and treated. I've never met an alcoholic who hasn't experienced periods of depression and anxiety, and severe episodes of this type are increasingly unavoidable with late-stage disease. But getting a prescription for drugs like Vicodin, a powerful painkiller, or Xanax, a popular tranquilizer, could be a recipe for disaster to an alcoholic. The physician's warning not to drink while taking such medications is like asking the addict not to breathe; and mixing these drugs with alcohol often leads to tragedy. At best, the person will replace one form of dependency with another. A more likely outcome is that he or she will become addicted to yet another substance in addition to the previous drug of choice. If a doctor prescribes a tranquilizer, painkiller or even an antidepressant to a recovering alcoholic, that should be questioned in the context of his/her substance abuse.

Years of experience have taught us that total abstinence from all mood-altering drugs is the only sure way to achieve long-term recovery. This necessarily involves an ongoing, daily process, one that requires continuing care, vigilance and support from loved ones and others who are in a position to help. *Achieving a program of recovery involves far more than not drinking.* As many thousands of people in recovery know, it is a way of life, one that has its rewards but also makes demands on us. I don't know of anyone who has been able to stay clean and sober alone. I often tell family members, "We need to do it for ourselves, but we can't do it by ourselves."

THE STIGMA OF THE "DRUNK" OR "JUNKIE"

The prospect of caring for someone through any illness can be daunting, but in our society when it comes to chemical dependency there is a double standard that can deter us from offering any assistance at all. The disease raises issues of privacy, personal rights and loyalty. The stigma associated with the illness often discourages potential caregivers from becoming involved.

If you live in the suburbs, you might see a man driving home from work, and as he approaches his house, he sees a neighbor down on hands and knees in the driveway. The neighbor's face is red and he's gasping. The guy on his way home immediately stops to help. You see him loosen the fellow's tie and then rush into the house to call for an ambulance. Now if you take the same scenario and put a bottle or a plastic bag next to this guy on his hands and knees, that same Good Samaritan will drive right past, go into his house, close the drapes and hope the neighbor didn't see him. The fellow will go out of his way to avoid the situation and explain to his wife, "Oh, Harry's just drunk again." The wife may say, "Well, maybe we should do something." And the husband will typically dismiss the idea by insisting, "It's none of our business."

Of course, making it your business to help can mean interfering in someone's private life, and this is a genuine concern for many people. Most of us were brought up to respect the privacy of others. An effort to intervene may seem like a rude or inappropriate intrusion. But if you care about someone with a disease, *common sense dictates that you consider the consequences of doing nothing.* In all cases of chemical dependency, when left untreated, the odds are simply overwhelming that the person will crash and burn, whether physically, emotionally or economically. Should the person be abandoned and left alone to deal with his illness? Viewed in this light, taking action to help is actually a profound act of compassion.

CHAPTER ONE
SUMMARY POINTS

The disease of chemical dependency is describable across a broad population and possesses the following characteristics:

1. It is a *primary disease* that causes and aggravates other mental and physical disorders.

2. It is a *chronic*, permanent condition that does not go away.

3. It is *progressive*—the disease follows a predictable course and worsens over time.

4. It is *fatal*—left untreated, the disease causes premature death.

5. It is *treatable*—the progression of the disease can be arrested by total abstinence from mood-altering drugs.

CHAPTER TWO

SIGNS AND SYMPTOMS OF CHEMICAL DEPENDENCY

DIAGNOSING THE DISEASE

If you suspect a person has a problem with alcohol or drugs, it's almost a certainty that he or she does. Most of the calls that I receive in my practice turn out to be much more serious situations than anyone imagined. Many of the people I see actually have late-stage disease, but they have managed to deceive those around them into seeing only the tip of their iceberg. The person in question may be drinking two six-packs at night, but downing six scotches before coming home from work. He or she may be doing great on the job as far as the family knows, but when that person sits down with me, I usually hear a different story—"I have to tell you I'm on probation at work. And I've got a couple of DWI's. I haven't told my wife yet."

Not only does the alcoholic not want the family to know that he or she has a problem, the family, too, doesn't want to believe there is a problem. Some spouses even work to sabotage an intervention.

CASE NOTES: THE DAUGHTER-IN-LAW

This case was set in motion by the parents of a using son. Their son's wife had become the breadwinner and may have felt more important when her husband used. She told me that my intervention wasn't necessary—her husband just concluded a big deal three months ago. Upon investigation, it turned out to be three years ago. Now, I had explained to the wife that the advantage comes to the interventionist when he catches the patient off guard—by surprise—so that they don't have time to build their defenses. I called her on her cell phone to determine the best time for me to come to the home. However, when I reached her, she nonchalantly called her husband (the user) over to the phone and said, "Honey, there's someone here who wants to speak with you!" That faux pas resulted in an additional two months of agony for her husband before I could get him into treatment.

Both husband and wife will often continue to live in a state of denial until some destructive crisis or a pattern of inappropriate behavior makes itself felt. In the same way, friends and employers are inclined to turn a blind eye to the early signs and symptoms of chemical dependency. Excuses for the alcoholic will be made by everyone, but sooner or later the problem will become impossible to ignore. Even after suspicions have been aroused, the "none of my business" rationalization may prevent anyone from openly confronting the person. The alcoholic will take advantage of the uncertainties and reticence of all those who might otherwise make an effort to help.

There is a simple litmus test for determining whether or not someone is suffering from chemical dependency: *If alcohol or drug use repeatedly disrupts a person's personal and social life, and if the person does not stop drinking or using, then he or she is chemically dependent.* The inability to quit drinking or using, even when it is having an ongoing, negative impact on a person's life, is a strong indication that the person is dependent on alcohol or drugs. As one of my early mentors once put it to me, *"An alcoholic will drink or use even when past experience, prudence and logic prohibit it."*

Dependency is most apparent when an individual refuses to stop using even after repeated disruptions of life. These disruptions can take any number of forms. There may be DWI arrests or other run-ins with the law. There may be conflicts with family and friends or reprimands from employers and teachers. While the non-alcoholic may go astray with a single drinking or drug incident that precipitates such a disruption, that one unpleasant episode will usually be enough to cause the non-alcoholic to take stock and alter his or her behavior. The person may simply say, "I've had enough of this grief!" and stop drinking and using altogether. By contrast, the alcoholic will continue to use. He or she may stop or cut down temporarily, sometimes for months or even years, but sooner or later there will be a recurrence and the habitual pattern of chemical abuse will reassert itself.

For the alcoholic, all personal relationships become secondary to drinking and using. Whatever his or her preferred substance may be, it is the ultimate priority in life, regardless of the painful disruptions and crises that it brings about. Compulsive attachment to the drug will cause the alcoholic to sacrifice any relationship that gets in the way of continued use. Abstinent friends will be replaced by those who use. Activities and pastimes that were important in the past will fall by the wayside. As the chemical increasingly takes on the power of a god, the addict becomes more and more incapable of acting on any genuine feelings of love and affection. Of course, such behavior is irrational and indicates, in no uncertain terms, the presence of the disease.

However close you may be to an alcoholic, you are probably seeing only a small part of the person's behavior, and you may be unaware of any past history of abuse. For example, a person you know may be arrested for a DWI and have no previous record. Drunk driving might seem entirely out of character. But he or she may have been driving under the influence dozens or hundreds of times in the past without being caught and without anyone knowing about it. The non-alcoholic is not likely to have three gin and tonics at a Christmas party and then be pulled over on the way home. That sort of mishap can happen, but it's really the exceptional case. When it does occur, the non-alcoholic will take responsibility and never allow it to happen again. At best, the alcoholic will try to be more careful about not getting caught the next time.

SYMPTOMS OF CHEMICAL DEPENDENCE

There are a number of symptoms of chemical dependency that often appear together and should enable you to clearly identify the disease. As you begin to understand how the illness progresses and how it affects its victims, its characteristics will become more apparent and recognizable. Some of the warning signs are hard to miss, though the alcoholic will make every effort to conceal them. Other clues are less conclusive by themselves and need to be considered within the larger picture. The process of diagnosis comes down to knowing what you are looking for and identifying an ongoing pattern of behavior. The key may not be a single calamity or crisis in someone's life, but rather a series of disruptions and behavioral changes that defy any other reasonable explanation.

While any list of symptoms is limited, the following observations are often related to me by my clients and may help you to confirm your suspicions. Keep in mind that no isolated symptom by itself can definitively establish the case for chemical dependency. It is usually a combination of symptoms that is most telling.

1. The person's need for alcohol or other drugs has increased, and he or she appears to be drinking or using more now than previously, to the point that you have reason to be concerned when the person is drinking and using.

2. The person's behavior while under the influence makes you uncomfortable, embarrassed, or fearful of being the object of his or her verbal or physical abuse.

3. The person increasingly looks forward to the next drinking or using episode—he or she may express an urgent need for that first drink of the day.

4. The person experiences memory blackouts—there are things that he or she forgets or denies that occurred during periods of drinking or using.

5. The person becomes annoyed, defensive or hostile when the subject of his or her drinking or drug use is brought up—the person may blame you or make excuses to rationalize his or her drinking or using.

6. The person exhibits physical tremors due to withdrawal—the person's hands will visibly shake before he or she has the first drink of the day.

7. The person drinks or uses in the morning to satisfy his or her need for the drug when there is obviously no social reason for drinking or using at that hour.

8. The person undergoes noticeable personality changes when under the influence—an otherwise quiet person may become loud and boisterous; a normally easygoing person may become argumentative and belligerent.

9. The person's behavior changes over time—he or she may become withdrawn, cynical, negative, erratic and undependable, losing interest in areas that were previously important, such as the well-being of loved ones and family activities.

10. The person avoids or complains about social events during which drinking or using will not be allowed—this can apply to social functions ranging from family gatherings where no alcohol is served to the enforced abstinence of sitting through a movie or concert.

11. The person is drinking or using surreptitiously—you may have caught the person hiding alcohol or drugs in the home or on the job.

12. The person asks you to lie or make excuses to others in order to cover up his or her drinking or using.

13. The person has repeatedly broken promises to quit drinking or using.

14. The person drives under the influence—he or she may have been arrested for DWI or DUI violations. The intoxicated person may stubbornly refuse the help of a designated driver.

15. The person is increasingly moody, anxious and depressed—he or she may exhibit low self-esteem to the point of self-loathing. The person may project his or her bitterness by lashing out at you and others, and afterwards, he or she might express remorse or guilt.

16. The person has financial and/or job difficulties that are caused by the use of alcohol or drugs.

17. The person's children or other family members are fearful when he or she is drinking or using.

18. The person increasingly avoids abstinent friends and prefers to socialize with people who are drinkers or drug users.

19. The person boasts about his tolerance for alcohol or other drugs and insists that he can control his drinking or using.

20. The person's thinking is increasingly muddled and irrational—he or she repeatedly exercises poor judgment.

Signs of Chemical Dependency in the Workplace

In the workplace, chemical dependency causes performance and attendance problems, as well as affecting conduct and relationships on the job. Employers and supervisors should be on the lookout for the following signs over time in combination:

1. Frequent tardiness and unauthorized absences.

2. Repeated excuses for missing work and excessive use of sick leave.

3. Missed deadlines and incomplete work assignments.

4. Careless, faulty work.

5. Failing to meet production quotas.

6. Strained relationships with fellow workers.

7. The employee may be short-tempered and belligerent, especially during the morning hours and after weekends.

8. The employee may be borrowing money from other employees or receiving phone calls at the workplace from creditors.

9. The employee may smell of alcohol, have bloodshot eyes, or exhibit tremors.

10. The employee may exhibit inappropriate mood and behavioral changes.

11. The employee may avoid supervisors, especially after lunch.

12. The employee may be obviously inebriated on the job or may fall asleep while on duty.

Alcoholics come in all colors, shapes and sizes, and their personal preferences and habits vary widely when it comes to their drug of choice. There are those who only drink beer or wine, and there are those who drink only on weekends. Others go on prolonged binges a few times a year. Some drug users will tell you that they are in no danger of becoming addicted because they use only marijuana or seemingly harmless diet pills. The frequency of use and the amount of alcohol or drugs consumed are often not as revealing and reliable as the behavioral indicators of dependency. Again, it is the inability or refusal to quit using—even after harmful, disruptive effects are felt in a person's life—that most clearly distinguishes the alcoholic from the non-alcoholic.

Given the alcoholic's ability to conceal and deny the problem, you may still have doubts about whether or not the person is chemically dependent. I usually advise my clients to trust their suspicions because it is far better to err on the side of caution. Suppose you have an athletic husband in his forties with no history of health problems. The fellow regularly works out and plays racquetball. One Saturday afternoon he and his family go to a football game, and they put down the tailgate and have a few drinks. They eat pizza, and everybody has a great time. But that night the fellow complains about chest pains. Should his family assume that he has indigestion? Or should they consult a doctor about the possibility of a heart problem? Isn't it safer to have a cardiologist be the one to suggest that he lay off the anchovies?

The same caution should be exercised when there is any question of alcoholism. If you continue to have uncertainties, you may want to consult a professional who specializes in chemical dependency. You can obtain referrals and counseling from most treatment centers and from the Twelve Step organizations such as Alcoholics Anonymous and Al-Anon. Whatever your situation may be, you will find that help is available if you make the effort to seek it out.

CHAPTER TWO
SUMMARY POINTS

Chemical dependency is characterized by an inability to stop drinking or using even after a person's life is disrupted by alcohol or drugs. Key symptoms of the disease include:

1. Loss of control and blackouts.

2. Personality changes and depression.

3. Inappropriate and destructive behavior.

4. Preoccupation with alcohol and drug use.

5. Failed attempts to quit drinking or using.

6. Accidents caused by alcohol or drugs.

7. Driving under the influence.

Chemical dependency can affect all areas of a person's life:

1. Family life.

2. Social relationships.

3. Religious or spiritual life.

4. Physical or emotional health.

5. Business or work efficiency.

6. Academic performance.

7. Financial stability.

CHAPTER THREE

How Chemical Dependency Progresses and Controls Its Victims

The Disease Affects Everyone

Alcohol and drug use are so widespread in our society that if a person is vulnerable to chemical dependency, he or she is almost sure to contract the disease. To put it another way, when the potential alcoholic starts to slide, the world is greased for the occasion. The disease gets its start when the individual is first introduced to social drinking or experiments with other drugs, whether these are obtained illegally or prescribed by a physician. Obviously, children are exposed to temptations from an early age, and the illness claims a growing number of youthful victims, even with our best efforts to caution and educate them about the dangers. But the other end of the age scale is also vulnerable, as is every age bracket in between. Addiction is a very patient disease and in some cases it will wait many years before becoming active and life-threatening.

As we have seen, what sets chemical dependency apart from most other diseases is the fact that its victims usually do not seek treatment on their own because they are unaware that they have the illness, even after its symptoms appear. The characteristic delusions and emotional impact associated with the disease prevent the person from being conscious of or accepting the fact that he or she is sick. This denial of reality is further complicated by the insidious way the disease affects both the alcoholic and those around him or her.

43

From the outset, the illness triggers feelings and attitudes that block both the alcoholic's ability to seek help and the ability of others to provide care. By understanding how the disease progresses, you will be better able to avoid the traps that we alcoholics set to keep you and others just as confused and paralyzed as we are.

STAGE ONE: INITIATION AND ADAPTATION

Whatever the particular drug of choice may be, it is perceived by the alcoholic as a "friend" from the beginning. There is a euphoric high that comes with the initial drinking or drug episode. Regardless of how the person felt before, that first drink makes him or her feel better. The alcoholic learns almost immediately that he or she can depend on the chemical to elevate mood. Further experience quickly teaches the person that the degree and duration of this happy mood swing can be controlled by increasing the amount consumed—the more the person drinks or uses, the better he or she feels, and the longer the feeling lasts. The drug can alleviate tension and instill a sense of well-being and confidence. The person may feel elated or giddy. In many cases, a shy, socially inhibited person will become more outgoing. He or she may be the fun-loving "life of the party" while under the influence and then return to normal after the effects of the drug wear off.

This first stage of chemical dependency can seem entirely harmless. There are as yet no emotional or social costs associated with the person's drinking or using. And there is nothing in the experience so far that differentiates the alcoholic from the normal social drinker. But, sooner or later, the afflicted person will start to actively pursue these chemically induced mood swings. At first, this might appear as innocent as the ritual of having two or three drinks after work just to take the edge off and relieve the stresses of the day. But two or three drinks for the alcoholic will eventually lead to four or five, with each intensifying the experience and carrying the person further down the slippery slope.

The habitual pattern of use can take any number of forms early on. The person might remain abstinent during the work week and look forward to weekend drinking episodes when he or she can cut loose from the daily routine. The person might drink only on holidays or special occasions, perhaps only a few times a year. The alcohol might be beer, wine or distilled spirits such as gin or scotch. The initiation process with alcohol is essentially equivalent to that of other drugs, with the drinks corresponding to marijuana joints, pills, lines of cocaine and so forth. Each substance causes its own unique alteration of mood. But whether characterized as a depressant, a stimulant, a psychedelic—whatever it may be—there is always the probability of dependency.

As the chemical becomes more established in the addict's life, he or she will come to believe in its power to alleviate emotional distress and to provide that welcome boost to his or her psyche. Eventually, belief in the drug will be absolute to point that the afflicted person comes to believe that life is not worth living without it. But, for now, the mood swings are pleasurable interludes without any serious drawbacks, and the seemingly benign power of the drug is reconfirmed each time the person finds relief in this way. The early drug experiences are deeply ingrained and stay with the person for a lifetime. The individual enjoys drinking at this point even if an occasional hangover makes the day after less than pleasant. Of course, a hangover will cause some physical pain—headache, nausea, and dehydration—but the discomfort is temporary and does not exact any serious emotional toll. The person may say,

"I drank too much last night, but it was worth it because I had such a good time."

The initial honeymoon phase of chemical dependency can last for weeks, months or years. Many drinkers never progress beyond this stage. They may continue to indulge but under appropriate circumstances and usually in moderation. The alcoholic, on the other hand, will inevitably graduate to a second phase of use during which the first harmful effects of dependency are felt.

STAGE TWO: DESTRUCTIVE DEPENDENCY

The second stage begins when the person drinks or uses to excess and exhibits some form of inappropriate behavior that has a definite emotional cost. The person's drinking will cause some untoward incident with personal repercussions. It may be an insult delivered at a party or a fight in a bar. It may be some wildly bizarre or potentially dangerous act. It may be a silly stunt like the proverbial lampshade on the head. But whatever form it takes, it will leave the person feeling worse than before, often embarrassed or ashamed. And for the first time, he or she will not return to normal after the effects of the drug wear off.

What is normal as far as mood, disposition and personality will change for the worse as the person adapts his or her behavior and lifestyle to accommodate the drug. The changes can take place slowly and may not be perceptible at first to the addict or to others. The habitual pattern of use will become more inflexible, and the person will look forward to the next drinking or using episode with an increasing sense of anticipation. If his or her drinking usually starts at the end of the work day, the alcoholic will be looking ahead to that first drink throughout the day. He or she may be in a business meeting and be distracted counting down the minutes on the clock. As time drags on, the person may become increasingly impatient and irritable, and might say or do anything just to bring the meeting to a close.

Once the drinking or using routine is established, the alcoholic will not allow anything to interfere with it. Any interruption or delay is likely to be met with resentment or annoyance. And anyone who gets in the way of that first drink of the day may be in for some measure of abuse. There may be temper tantrums or even violent outbursts. The person may become morose, sullen or overtly hostile when compelled to depart from his or her routine and forced to endure a period of abstinence.

The afflicted person's relationship with the chemical has now begun to take on an importance that rivals his or her social relationships. At the same time, the effects of the drug are subject to a diminishing rate of return. More of the drug is now required to achieve that same euphoric boost, and the person needs the first drink earlier in the day. As the alcoholic's tolerance rises, he or she will drink or use more to try to recapture the high as he or she first experienced it. The person who can drink you under the table is usually able to do so simply because he or she needs to consume more than you to become inebriated.

We alcoholics are world champions when it comes to tolerance, and whenever we show off our ability to hold our liquor, we are also liable to walk or stumble into one of those compromising situations that disrupt our lives. Yet those disruptive incidents, even when they become more frequent and serious, will not deter us from drinking and using again. In fact, the drug is our only way to mentally escape the fallout of our behavioral lapses. When we lose a job or find ourselves in conflict with family or friends, we will turn to the chemical and its mood shift to try to blot out the emotional cost, if only temporarily.

The more that we come to depend on the drug in this way, the more clever we are at obtaining it and concealing our use of it. And the more ingenious we become at rationalizing our behavior. The rationalizations are subconscious, and the more we believe them, the more deluded and out of touch with reality we are. We have to deceive ourselves because the truth, especially as it relates to our using, is far too threatening and disturbing for us to accept consciously. We therefore twist the facts to avoid the painful aspects of our existence and to justify our continued use. We will tell you, "I would never have said or done such a thing." And we will insist again and again, "I can handle my drinking. Just stay out of it!" The denials and delusions have now become a way of life.

STAGE THREE: DETERIORATION

With the third and final stage of chemical dependency, the emotional price that we have been paying for our behavior finally catches up with us. We are more and more consumed by feelings of remorse, guilt, anxiety and shame. We carry these feelings with us day in and day out and try to hold them at bay the only way that we know how—by turning to the drug for relief. By now we may not even be able to start the day without our chemical friend. We want to feel good again, but at this point we are drinking or using just to try to feel normal. In fact, we have no choice but to drink or use because we are in such anguish that we can hardly bear to be sober anymore.

We feel miserable now even when we are under the influence. Things that mattered to us in the past have less or no importance, from our social relationships to our jobs. Even

48

our personal hygiene may be neglected. Life for us has become a continuing series of setbacks and reversals. Our egos have been battered by failure and rejection. Our self-esteem has been chipped away with each self-demeaning act. We are ruled by our negative emotions and all of these contribute to a growing sense of self-hatred. There may be prolonged periods of depression and suicidal impulses. We are often afraid that we are going to die, but also afraid that we won't die, imagining that we have somehow been condemned to live in this state of constant emotional agony. As we continue to decline, the condition can become what is known as chronic *alcoholic depression*, a frequent cause of suicide.

Late-stage alcoholics will put up with almost any degree of discomfort rather than seek to change their behavior.

Case Notes: The Disappearing Executive

I was once called in to help a mid-level executive who had the habit of disappearing without notice. He would come into the office to collect his paycheck while his bosses were out, and then he would vanish. As it turned out, the fellow had made a home for himself in a friend's backyard. He was sleeping in a tiny tool shed, in the middle of January no less. After the intervention, while he and I were traveling to a treatment center, we discussed his unusual lodgings. He told me, "It wasn't so bad. I had blankets and a portable radio. In the morning, I washed and shaved at a gas station." Apparently, the only aspect of his existence that bothered him was not being able to fit his entire body inside the shelter. From the knees down, he was exposed to the elements. Once when he was drunk, he passed out in the reverse position with his upper body out in the snow. This man has since become a sober friend and active member in the AA program.

Affluent alcoholics exhibit the same stubbornness, and if the situation were not so tragic it might appear humorous.

Case Notes: Room Service

I worked with one wealthy alcoholic whose wife, a savvy southern lady, constantly nagged him to stop drinking. The husband finally moved out and took up residence in a beautiful hotel near their home. He immediately began tipping the bellmen to keep him supplied with booze. The wife soon caught on and began tipping the bellmen not to bring booze to her husband. This bidding war went on until my intervention brought the fellow into treatment, which probably saved the couple a great deal of money.

Many alcoholics experience memory blackouts, which can occur during earlier stages as well. The person will forget or repress events that happened while drinking or using. These memory lapses are a form of amnesia caused by the drug, and they can last for hours or even days. While in a blackout episode, the alcoholic may appear to be functioning normally. The person can engage in any activity that he or she might otherwise do—drive a car, fly a plane, attend a business meeting, perform surgery, etc. But afterwards, the alcoholic will have no recollection of anything that occurred during the blackout period.

At the time that we decide to put the lampshade on our head, we know what we are doing. We know how to unscrew the little cap on top of the lamp so the shade will come off and we can put it on our head. But the next day we will have no memory of our antics with the shade. Likewise, we know how to get in the car, start it and put it into gear. But later we don't remember driving and hitting that child who was crossing the street. The memory loss is permanent and not dependent on how much we were drinking or using. Even a small amount of alcohol or drugs can trigger a blackout.

Blackouts are disorienting and cause further anxiety as the disease progresses and they become more frequent. Typically, the alcoholic will try to cover up these disturbing episodes, but first he or she has to find out what actually happened from someone who witnessed the event. A husband may ask his wife over coffee the next morning, "Well, what did you think of the party last night?" If she brings up some outrageous behavior on his part that he has blacked out, he may deny his actions and discredit her account of the evening. We alcoholics will always try to put you at the disadvantage even as ludicrous as our denials may be when we can't even remember what took place.

Case Notes: "I did what?!"

I once worked with an alcoholic lawyer who had been vacationing with his family at an ocean resort. He woke up one morning covered with scraped skin from his nose to his feet. The day before his family found him trying to take a swim in the driveway in front of his beach house. When he was told about the incident, his response was an incredulous "I did what?" I also intervened with a fellow who had been under the influence of LSD when he crushed a man against a wall with his car. When the police later arrested him and told him what he had done, he too reacted with shocked disbelief. "I did what!"

We also distort our memories in another way: we remember how we felt under the influence but not how we actually behaved. If we were slurring our words and stumbling the night before, we will recall being in complete control and fiercely deny your accusations that we were drunk. We trust our distorted memories even though we have no ability to evaluate our own condition while we are drinking and using. Because of the false confidence instilled by the drug, we delude ourselves into believing that we have the ability to function normally, or even better than we would otherwise. People really believe that they drive better, or make love better, or do business better when they are drinking or using. I've had alcoholic clients who were Wall Street brokers, and before entering treatment, they often insist, "I'm much better trading on the floor when I've done a line of coke and had a few drinks with lunch."

All the while our emotional and personal lives are deteriorating, we will unconsciously project our self-loathing and all our negative feelings onto you and others, often by going on the attack and lashing out. We hate ourselves and take it out on you. We will arrogantly blame everyone around us for our ongoing misery. We mistrust even our closest friends. As our fears multiply, we become increasingly paranoid. The most innocent remark from someone we know can be interpreted as a slight or betrayal, and we will magnify it and dissect it for weeks, replaying it over and over in our minds. We live each day wondering who knows what about our using. Who did my wife tell? Did my kids say anything? Does my boss know? Such questions become mentally all-consuming. Many alcoholics live with a sense of impending doom, and with late stage disease, that feeling is often more than justified.

The physical symptoms of chemical dependency also appear during this final stage. Before more serious conditions such as liver or heart disease present themselves, there are usually other signs of debilitation. Addicts may gain or lose weight because of improper diet related to their drinking and using. Because dependence on the drug is physical as well as psychological, the addict may exhibit withdrawal symptoms during brief periods of abstinence. The alcoholic's hands will shake before he or she has that first drink of the day. Once again, denial comes into play. If someone happens to notice the person's trembling hands, the alcoholic may complain about cold weather or concoct some other lame excuse.

Keep in mind that it is impossible to predict how rapidly the disease will progress, and this can make the early and late stages of the disease difficult to distinguish. In addition, the symptoms can vary from person to person and don't appear all at once. If on your first date with an alcoholic, he or she were to get drunk, punch you in the mouth, and then leave you stranded on the highway with no money, would you go out with this person again? It usually doesn't happen that way. At first, it's a few drinks and a lot of harmless fun, and then the disease kicks in and the person's life gradually falls apart.

As difficult as it may be for you to accept, the fact is that we alcoholics remain totally unaware of the progression of the disease even as the symptoms become more severe and we watch our lives spin further out of our control. The rationalizations, projections, blackouts and mental aberrations continue to blind us to our condition. After treatment, many of my clients express shock at how they and those around them allowed the situation to get so far out of hand. With hindsight, they will often ask, "Why did I wait so long to clean up my act? Why didn't someone step in and help me years ago?"

One of the reasons that no one is inclined to take action, in most cases, is that the alcoholic's emotional tailspin pulls everyone into the malaise. The people who are closest to the afflicted person, especially family members and loved ones, cannot avoid being deeply affected by his or her behavior. To some extent, all of those who come into contact with the alcoholic are drawn into the person's emotional and delusional syndrome. Whatever the specific circumstances of your own situation may be, you are probably experiencing many of the same feelings that the alcoholic in your life is experiencing. You will need to understand and address those feelings before any real progress can be made.

How the Chemically Dependent Person Affects You

As we respond to our pain, we alcoholics experience a veritable buffet of feelings. We succumb to the entire gamut of negative emotions. While the disease may not be contagious, the feelings are. Through our actions and loss of control over our behavior, we cause others to feel the same hurt, fear, anger, anxiety, shame, guilt, despair and loneliness that we are feeling. Because you are close to the afflicted person, you are probably experiencing many of the emotional symptoms of the disease even without being chemically dependent yourself.

If you have been repeatedly hurt and violated by the alcoholic in your life, it is likely that you have been unable to separate the person from his or her illness. Instead of seeing the person as sick, you think of him or her as being willfully malicious. You may feel a confused mixture of love and hate because of the history of his or her behavior toward you. It may not be easy for you to accept the fact that the person's hurtful actions are not deliberate, but the involuntary outcome of his or her dependency. Only by examining your own feelings can you begin to deal with them and prepare yourself to come to grips with the person's illness.

Any number of the following emotional scenarios might apply to you:

- You feel ashamed for the person because he or she has embarrassed you in front of your family, friends or employer. If the person is your spouse, he or she may have caused you to feel ashamed of yourself just for being married to someone who behaves so outrageously and irresponsibly.

- You feel guilty because you mistakenly believe that you have caused the person's illness or that you are in some way responsible for it. You may feel a sense of guilt because all your efforts to help have failed. Every time you have tried to get the person to face the problem, you have met with accusations that his or her drinking or using is your fault.

- You feel powerless and fearful of the person. You are afraid for yourself and your family whenever her or she drinks or uses. The person is verbally or physically abusive and puts you and others in danger. You never know when he or she will explode and the next ugly scene will occur.

- You feel angry because of the way the person has mistreated you. You are furious with the person and deeply resentful of his or her abusiveness. You are caught in a vicious circle of escalating anger, blame and recrimination. You may be tempted to seek revenge to make the person pay for the grief that he or she has caused you.

- You feel depressed and down on yourself because the alcoholic constantly criticizes you and undermines your

self-esteem. You are repeatedly told what an awful person you are, that you are the one to blame for all of his
or her problems. The person attacks your masculinity or
femininity, your appearance, your intelligence, your talent, your attitude—every intimate detail of your life is
being used against you.

- You feel a growing sense of loneliness, of being unloved
  and unwanted. The person's lack of attentiveness and
  respect makes you feel isolated and cut off from your
  family and friends. He or she seems to speak a different
  language than you do, and you find it more and more
  difficult to communicate with the person or anyone else
  about the situation. You feel that you are alone in dealing with the problem and helpless to change the way
  things are.

- You don't know whether you will ever be able to forgive
  the person for the things that he or she has said and done
  to you. The person has crossed the line with behavior
  that is so hurtful that forgiveness on your part might
  seem impossible. You may be asking yourself how you
  could ever have loved or cared for such a person.

How Others Enable the Disease to Progress

The people around the chemically dependent person,
especially family members, usually adopt their own set of
defenses to shield themselves from the pain and all of the negative feelings that he or she causes. Those on the receiving end
of the person's reckless and abusive behavior can play a number of defensive roles that are all ultimately self-defeating and
actually enable the person to continue drinking and using. We
alcoholics will turn your best intentions against you and make

you unwittingly complicit with us in allowing the disease to progress.

Case Notes: Some Lines for the Road

I once intervened with a clever young female cocaine addict, and her parents insisted that they should be the ones to drive her several hundred miles to the treatment center. They wanted to be certain that she remained clean during the trip. Before leaving, the young woman told her mother and father that she needed money to pay her drug dealer because he was threatening her. The parents agreed and drove to the dealer's house. Unwittingly, they gave their daughter money to pay the dealer. As you might expect, she went into the house and bought a sufficient supply of cocaine to last her during their trip.

Typically, those around the alcoholic step into support roles during the early stage of the disease when the person first begins to drink or use excessively and exhibits some form of inappropriate behavior. Everyone wants to avoid suffering any consequences that arise from someone else's drug abuse. A husband or wife will make excuses or apologize to other family members and outsiders for the mishaps caused by the spouse. The wife may lie to cover up for her drunk or hungover husband by calling his boss to say that he has the flu and can't come to work. She knows the bills have to be paid and doesn't want him to lose his job. But she is only postponing the inevitable. As the disease progresses, she will run out of excuses and, sooner or later, he will lose that job anyway.

Each time you make excuses or offer apologies on behalf of the chemically dependent person, you step into the defensive role of *protecting* him or her from the harmful effects of the disease. As innocent as this might seem, you are allowing the illness to progress and helping the alcoholic to conceal the problem. You may buy into his or her rationalizations by telling yourself that everyone drinks too much on occasion, that this is just a phase he or she is going through. In this way, you are sharing his or her delusion. You may prevail upon the person to promise that he or she will quit drinking or using, but time will prove that the alcoholic's promises are worthless. In reality, you cannot protect the person from the disease, and each time you attempt to do so, you compromise yourself and both of you are victimized. As your efforts to protect the addict prove more and more futile, you are likely to blame yourself and experience feelings of inadequacy, shame and guilt. When this happens, your own self-image is bound to suffer.

Many family members who try to protect the alcoholic also try in various ways to control or manage his or her drinking or using. For example, a wife may drink with her husband to try to limit his consumption. She might take over the buying of alcoholic beverages in order to keep tabs on purchases and to reduce his drinking at home. She may try to avoid social gatherings that are likely to encourage her husband's drinking. She may throw out liquor or drugs that her husband has hidden. In the long run, such efforts by family members to control the alcoholic's consumption are destined to fail, and the would-be controller usually ends up taking that failure personally as yet another sign of his or her inadequacy.

Those who attempt to protect and control the alcoholic are often trying to compensate for the person's behavior. They desperately want to keep everyone else happy and unaware of the problem. They will try to defuse any uncomfortable or potentially embarrassing situation with humor or by distracting attention away from the chemically dependent person. Like the gracious host who tries to make sure that everybody has a great time, the non-using friend or loved one will go out of the way to fulfill the expectations of others and allay concerns about the alcoholic. To this end, family members will often attempt to be exemplary or perfect in their everyday social roles. They try to put themselves beyond reproach to make up for the alcoholic's antisocial behavior.

You might try to be the ideal mate, the perfect husband or wife, the perfect parent, the perfect son or daughter. This was my experience as a child when I tried to compensate for my mother's alcoholism. When she had been drinking and was unable to get out of bed in the morning, I would dutifully cater to her needs and clean the house, without consciously realizing that anything was wrong. As time went on, I tried to please my parents by excelling in school and in sports, as if my achievements would somehow remedy my mother's condition.

Children, of course, are most vulnerable in thinking that the alcoholic's behavior is normal and must be accepted as such no matter how painful it may be. Rather than trying to appease an alcoholic parent as I did by overachieving, many children of alcoholics at some point rebel against the family. They become unruly and defiant. They resist authority at home and in school. They may themselves turn to alcohol or drugs. Whatever the individual reaction is during childhood and adolescence, later in life, the grown-up children of alcoholics often continue to suffer the consequences of the parent's disease. Until they address such issues through therapy or by some other means, many have chronic problems with self-image and social relationships.

Defensive roles in the family can take many forms,

depending on the circumstances and the personalities of those involved. Rather than protecting the alcoholic, family members may go to the opposite extreme by repeatedly blaming and attacking the afflicted person. When an alcoholic husband's behavior takes its toll on his wife's sense of self-worth, she may project her feelings of failure and inadequacy onto him and others. There may be verbal assaults, fits of temper and violent outbursts on both sides. The husband and wife will dump all their problems onto each other. Either spouse may threaten to leave or end the marriage. Despite the threats and hostilities, and even in those cases when the marriage does break up, the alcoholic's drinking or using will go on unabated. In my practice, I have seen that when breakups do occur, the alcoholic spouse will often be temporarily ecstatic, relieved of the nagging and free to drink or drug himself into oblivion.

Other self-defeating, defensive stances include variations on the theme of apathy and detachment. The sense of personal failure and feelings of inadequacy can cause a spouse or other family member to withdraw. He or she may refuse to participate in family activities. The previously outgoing person may become quiet and reticent to offer his or her opinion on any subject. This can be a form of passive aggression as the person cuts off family ties, spends more and more time alone, and rejects all other social relationships. The apathetic, detached person may seem to be outwardly without feelings while inside he or she is actually experiencing the same turmoil as those who act out their negative emotions.

All of the defensive roles taken by those surrounding the alcoholic—protecting, controlling, compensating, blaming, attacking, rebelling, withdrawing and so forth—can exist simultaneously. They are also essentially interchangeable. A single family member can play several roles at once.

The person can switch them on and off throughout the day. He or she may protect and control in the morning, blame and attack in the afternoon and then withdraw overnight. As misguided reactions to the disease, all of the roles have one thing in common: they enable the alcoholic to continue to drink or use. In fact, any type of defensive action that falls short of intervening to help the afflicted person get treatment ultimately enables the disease to progress.

The fact of the matter is that until the addict is confronted with the reality of his or her condition, he or she will fiercely resist and thwart all of your efforts to help. Many people try to intervene informally without having a specific plan of action. You may have insisted in the past that the person you know should seek help. You may have urged him or her to consider counseling, or Alcoholics Anonymous, or even clinical treatment. To appease you, the person may have gone to an AA meeting or made an appointment to see a therapist. Yet it is more than likely that the person is still drinking or using, still making excuses and still headed for catastrophe. The reason is that until the alcoholic actually identifies the reality of the illness, he or she will resort to the same bag of tricks to avoid giving up the drug. The person has managed to evade and foil your well-intentioned efforts before, and he or she will play for your sympathy and find a way to manipulate and deceive you again. The more we alcoholics are pressured and threatened, the more desperate and clever we become.

The only way to effectively deal with the problem is to understand the dynamics of the disease and to adopt a strategy to break its stranglehold once and for all. This will require commitment, planning and follow-through on your part in order to halt the progress of the disease and to put the person on the path to recovery. The process of intervention is like mounting a rescue operation. It is no small undertaking, and you may need professional help along the way, but such a plan can be carried out safely and effectively, step by step. If you have read this far, you realize the person is in urgent need of assistance. By entering into the planning stage of intervention, you will take a giant step toward reclaiming that person's life and health, and your own.

CHAPTER THREE
SUMMARY POINTS

How Chemical Dependency Progresses:

1. Stage One of the disease begins with relatively harmless drinking or drug use. The person is introduced to the chemical and learns how to control the mood swing it causes by increasing or limiting the amount consumed. He or she always returns to normal after the effects of the drug wear off.

2. Stage Two marks the onset of the first harmful effects of drinking or using. The person exhibits inappropriate or bizarre behavior for which there is an emotional cost. He or she no longer returns to a normal feeling state after drinking or using.

3. Stage Three is marked by worsening emotional torment, desperation, depression and potentially fatal drug-related diseases. The person experiences memory blackouts and physical tremors due to withdrawal. The person is no longer capable of feeling normal without drinking or using. He or she drinks and uses to avoid the anguish of being sober.

How Chemical Dependency
Affects Others:

1. Those close to the addict experience the same negative feelings as he or she does, including hurt, anger, shame, fear, guilt, despair, inadequacy and loneliness.

2. Family members adopt defensive roles to protect, control, blame, attack or withdraw from the addict.

3. The negative emotions, rationalizations and defensive roles of those close to the addict enable the progression of the disease to continue.

PART TWO

INTERVENTION, TREATMENT AND LONG-TERM RECOVERY

CHAPTER FOUR

INITIATING A PLAN OF ACTION

WHAT CAN YOU DO TODAY?

Before doing anything else, family members and other potential caregivers are strongly advised to break the pattern of their own previous behavior that may have facilitated drinking or using on the part of the chemically dependent person. Regardless of what enabling roles you may have been playing up until now—blaming, attacking, protecting, and so forth—you need to step back from the situation and adopt a new attitude and strategy for dealing with the afflicted person in your life.

Instead of reacting spontaneously to the person on the basis of your negative emotions, you can respond deliberately with a constructive plan of action. Instead of being victimized by the person's illness, you can take positive action to help him or her recover. By confronting the chemically dependent person in a responsible manner with the indisputable facts of his or her illness, the delusions and denials that have paralyzed both of you can be swept aside. Such a liberating moment of truth can be brought about through the process of intervention. As mentioned earlier, this procedure for confronting the person is not something meted out as a punishment. Nor should it be construed in any way as a personal attack. *An intervention is intended only to attack the illness, not the person suffering with it.*

You will need to prepare yourself in order to plan and initiate an intervention, whether it is conducted by a trained professional on your behalf or by a group that includes you and others like yourself who are close to the afflicted person. With professional guidance, the planning can be accomplished in a short time—days. Once the plan is set into motion, the goal of every intervention, whether carried out by an experienced intermediary or by you and a group of allies, is to motivate the person to accept treatment for his or her illness. Intervention and treatment are both essential in initiating the process of recovery.

With that goal in mind, there are a number of things that you can do immediately to lay the groundwork for a successful intervention. Changing your attitude and behavior along the following lines will allow the first glimmer of reality to break through the defenses that the person has relied on to defeat your efforts in the past:

- *Stop blaming.* By not criticizing and faulting the person for his or her illness, you can step outside the vicious circle of blaming each other for the problem.

- *Stop attacking.* By not provoking conflict or allowing yourself to be drawn into arguments, you can prevent the person from using you as an excuse to rationalize his or her drinking or using.

- *Stop protecting.* By not making any further excuses and apologies to cover up for the person's drinking or using, you can begin to make him or her aware of the consequences of the illness.

These immediate changes in the way that you relate to the alcoholic can have many practical implications depending on your specific relationship with the person. For example, prior to intervening on behalf of a wife with a chemically dependent husband, I will usually advise her, "Starting now, don't talk about his drinking or drug use anymore. Don't even mention it. Stop nagging, threatening, moaning or staring at him. If he comes in and pours himself a drink and you would normally say, 'Please don't start that again'—don't say it. Don't argue with him. Just ignore him."

What this does is break a pattern of behavior that has already proven futile. If she says nothing to him, that's a beginning—all of the sudden, the person goes on with his drinking or using, but his wife isn't commenting. This has an immediate effect. The atmosphere at home will change dramatically, and the husband's world of drinking or drugging will have been disrupted before the actual intervention is undertaken. In a sense, he is being put on notice, and his illness is being exposed. It's as if a spotlight were being thrown on the disease, making it more difficult for him to deny its reality.

In this regard, I also strongly advise the wife to stop making excuses for him. I may say to her, "Don't call your husband's boss and say that he's going to be late because he has a dead battery. Don't tell your kids that Daddy's working at the office and that's why he couldn't come to their football practice. Don't call your in-laws and say that he's sick and can't come to their picnic. Stop all of that. If you plan dinner for seven and he shows up at nine, don't make allowances for him. After you finish eating, just do the dishes and go about your business. If you would normally keep his pot roast warm, put it away. That kind of thing has been of zero value in the past, so there's no reason to think it will be of any value now. From now on, let your husband suffer the consequences of his drinking." *As long as there is a cushion, the drinker will drink and the user will use.*

In addition, I tell the wife that she will have to address her own alcohol or drug use. She will have to take an honest look at that part of the picture. Her own abstinence will strengthen her position and she can avoid playing any sort of enabling role as she proceeds. I will ask her to start a journal and write down everything—what he does, what he says, and how she feels. This kind of written documentation is critical in all cases, and, as we will see in the next chapter, the record of the afflicted person's behavior will be used to advantage during the intervention itself.

After working through this much of the plan with her in advance, I'll ask her to decide what she wants to do. Does she want to follow through with the intervention? I may say, "What if I didn't exist? What would you do if you thought the next ten years were going to be like this?" And she will often say, "I don't know, but I can't take it anymore." I'll ask her, "Does that mean you now want to leave your husband?" Maybe she does, or maybe she doesn't. She may be too fragile and confused to make a decision yet to help him or herself.

I'll ask her to take a few days to think about it. But usually the phone will ring within hours. She may still have doubts. She may say, "But I love him." And I'll ask her, "What is there to love, given the way things are? Do you love being abused? Do you love him vomiting on the floor at night? Do you love him disappearing for two or three days at a time? What do you love about this person?" She hates living this way, and she knows the situation will only get worse if she does nothing. And it will indeed take an act of love and courage to help him and her family. But she is the one who has to decide. It's her choice.

Depending on your own circumstances, this is the kind of difficult choice that you have to make as well. Whatever your specific relationship to the alcoholic is, you have a window of opportunity to intervene in a meaningful, effective way now that you have begun to educate yourself about the disease and have identified the problem for what it is. If you delay, that opportunity will soon be lost. The earlier you decide to intervene, the better. Over the years, various studies have suggested that if a chemically dependent person has not yet lost a job, destroyed a marriage or suffered some physical impairment, the person is more likely to be able to recover. Essentially, the less advanced the disease is at the time of treatment, the more readily treatable it is and the shorter the recovery time is likely to be.

As you convince yourself that intervention is the best course of action, the focus of your attention can shift to the practical and immediate steps that you can take to insure success. The decision to intervene is never an easy one to make, but if you allow your soul-searching to turn into endless procrastination and postponements, you will only be placing that person's life and health further into jeopardy.

I often ask reluctant clients, "How sick do you want him to get before you do something about it? Are you willing to stand by and watch him die and possibly kill you or someone else along the way? Why wait until he becomes more of an emotional and physical wreck than he already is?" (Supply the "she" where appropriate.)

OVERCOMING YOUR FEAR AND RELUCTANCE TO INTERVENE

Fear and reluctance are natural reactions that many people have at the prospect of carrying out an intervention. You may be afraid to confront the person or you may fear that you will somehow make the situation worse by attempting to intervene.

Case Notes: Never Too Late

I intervened with a lovely socialite of about 80 years of age. At first, her sons were reluctant to change her life, thinking they should let her live out her days as she wished, even if it meant as an alcoholic. But her youngest son was deeply concerned. He felt that his mom's quality of life was so poor—she was no longer invited to the luncheons and fund raisers; she no longer used her box at the ballet; her fantastic trips abroad were no more. He felt that his Mom was just a shell of the dynamo she once was, that she was lonely, and a change should be made. Just a few months after we intervened, she was back in the mainstream of the New York social scene and has been joyously sober for more than five years.

You may not believe that anything you do will help. You may be so angry and frustrated that you have reached the point of giving up on the person. Yet there is something that prevents you from turning your back and walking away from the problem. Perhaps you remember how things used to be before the person began drinking and using. Now is the time to ask yourself if you care enough to try to save his or her life. If your answer is yes, then you have no choice but to act decisively and without further delay.

You and others who know the afflicted person may think that by ignoring the problem, it will somehow go away by itself, or that something will happen to improve the situation. But if you've read this far, you now realize that chemical dependency is a disease that will inevitably get worse if not treated. Because you recognize the symptoms of the disease for what they are, it is no longer possible for you to accept the person's denials and rationalizations. When the alcoholic insists after a nightlong binge that he or she is no different from any other healthy, normal person who indulges on occasion, you can now see through that delusion. You know too much about the illness to ignore the problem any longer.

Nevertheless, you may be waiting because you believe that, sooner or later, the person will "hit bottom" and be compelled by some life-threatening crisis to seek help. It does happen in rare cases that the alcoholic's life deteriorates at some point in such a critical way that he or she may actually be forced into facing reality. When this occurs, the walls of the person's defenses may come crashing down, and out of sheer desperation he or she might reach out for help. But the chances of this happening are very slim. Why run such a terrible risk when you now know that the nature of the illness will in most cases prevent the alcoholic from even accepting the fact that he or she is sick? Again, the odds are overwhelming that the person will go on drinking or using until someone intervenes.

You may be asking yourself why that someone has to be you. Because you care for the person and have begun to educate yourself about the disease, you are probably better qualified than anyone else to initiate the process of intervention. While others may still be entrapped by the alcoholic's delusions and denials, you are in a position to set them straight. You will need allies along the way to support this rescue effort, and your firsthand knowledge of the situation will help win them over.

If you are uncomfortable about having to confront the afflicted person about his or her drug use, you can recruit a professional to intercede for you in planning and carrying out the actual face-to-face intervention. This option will be discussed in detail in the next chapter. Many of my clients prefer not to risk the potential conflicts that may ensue if they try to discuss the problem openly with the alcoholic during an intervention. They don't feel qualified to intervene on their own, but they care enough to get the expert help they need. I've been in many situations that turned out unexpectedly.

Case Notes: The Hotel Room

One intervention was to take place in a luxury New York hotel room. The father, a small, quiet man, was to take me up to the room and introduce me to his son, who was addicted to heroin, and leave us. When he opened the door, the father exploded. He saw his son using and "involved" with two prostitutes, who were also using. The old man exploded, shrieked and lunged for his son's throat. It was a terrible fight. I finally got them apart. The hotel security came. I dismissed the cast of characters and finally had the young man alone in the room where I did the intervention. It took two more months on the phone to get him into treatment. He did go to treatment and remains clean and sober.

If you are a friend or employer rather than a significant other or family member, you may feel uneasy about intruding or invading the person's privacy. But the bottom line is that whenever chemical dependency is treated as a private matter, the disease has its chance to progress and kill. Up until now, you may have thought it was the alcoholic's personal choice to drink or use, but as we have seen, the person actually has no choice at all when it comes to his or her addiction. Unless you overcome your reluctance, I can almost guarantee that you will be allowing and even encouraging a personal tragedy to play itself before your eyes.

Regardless of how close you are to the alcoholic, you may be uncomfortable initially with what you might see as going behind the person's back in order to plan an intervention. But by talking to others about the person's behavior, by comparing notes and agreeing on a definite course of action, you will actually be preparing in the most honest way to bring the problem into the open. Eventually, your preparations will be made known to the alcoholic and may be used during the intervention itself to make the case that he or she needs to go into treatment. If you are concerned about what the person's reaction will be afterwards, I can tell you this much: *I have never had anyone come back to me wishing that I had not intervened.* The usual response is one of gratitude to all those who cared enough to get the person help.

There is nothing secretive or underhanded about an intervention. Everyone who participates directly or indirectly is contributing to the only healthy solution available for the alcoholic's problem. For many who take part, it comes as a wonderful relief just to clear the air for the first time. When an intervention is properly conducted, family members and friends can talk about what has been happening in their lives and express their feelings about the person in a caring, constructive fashion. As an act of shared compassion and good will, the experience often turns out to be a cathartic release that starts the emotional healing process for all involved.

An intervention cannot be undertaken alone because the alcoholic's defenses are too strong to be overcome by one person. Even when I intervene privately with someone, I always have the assistance of the family or others who engage my services, although they are not present when I intervene. If you have decided to pursue the course of intervention, you will need a confidante in the planning stage to support your efforts. A confidante should be someone you trust, someone who will not be prejudiced or judgmental—a close friend or relative, a member of the clergy, a doctor, a lawyer, a teacher, someone secure in his or her own recovery, or someone who has experience in dealing with alcohol or drug problems. With the aid of such a person, you can begin to decide how, when and where the intervention can take place, who should participate and who should play the lead role in conducting the intervention.

The choice of a confidante is an important one and should not be taken lightly. It is not advisable to turn to the alcoholic's employer for help at this early stage, even if that person is a friend. The reason for this is to avoid any legal problems that might ensue if the alcoholic should lose a job because of your disclosure about his or her condition. Unfortunately, this can happen even with the best of intentions on all sides. Of course, there are situations where the employer is the one who takes on the active role of organizing the intervention, in which case, he or she may turn to the employee's co-workers and family for assistance.

As a professional interventionist, I am sometimes asked to approach an employer on behalf of my client, but this can only be done if the employer is already aware of the problem, or later, when the alcoholic has agreed to treatment. In these situations, the employer may be able to offer assistance through Human Resources and/or Employee Assistance Programs (EAP). If the company provides such benefits, an EAP counselor may be consulted. The attitudes of employers can vary considerably, but more and more realize that it is cost-effective to provide some form of support for employees whose performance on the job is impaired by alcohol and drugs.

Who Should Carry Out the Intervention?

The safest and most effective option is to have a qualified professional intervene on behalf of the family, friends or employer of the alcoholic. This approach is always advisable in cases when there is a history of mental illness or violence, abusive or reckless behavior, severe depression or addiction to multiple drugs. The layperson or amateur interventionist is not qualified to deal with such complications. A group intervention in these cases, even when conducted by a professional, is likely to degenerate into destructive clashes between the participants and the alcoholic. Potentially dangerous conflicts of this kind can be avoided by recruiting an experienced interventionist to intercede privately with the person, one-on-one, confidentially, without anyone else being present.

If you are fearful or insecure about carrying out the intervention on your own, you probably have good reason for your misgivings and should seek a professional to assist you. You may be temperamentally unsuited to lead the intervention but still be able to play an important support role. You will need to read ahead to find out exactly what the procedure entails in order to determine the best course for you to pursue, given your own personal limitations and the specific situation that you are facing. You may decide that you are capable of organizing an intervention without professional assistance. But before attempting to proceed on your own, you should carefully consider the cautionary advice in the next chapter based on my experience and the history of intervention as the practice has evolved during recent decades.

CHAPTER FOUR
SUMMARY POINTS

What can you do today?

1. Stop enabling the alcoholic to continue to drink and use.

2. Stop protecting the alcoholic by making excuses and offering apologies to others.

3. Stop blaming the alcoholic for his or her alcohol and drug use.

4. Stop attacking the alcoholic for problems related to his or her dependency.

5. Make the decision to intervene and start planning the intervention.

How can you overcome fear and reluctance to take action?

1. Remember if you do nothing, the alcoholic's condition will only worsen and create more serious problems for both of you.

2. Remind yourself that the alcoholic will die prematurely unless you act.

3. Recruit a confidante to support your effort to intervene.

4. Obtain professional advice as needed on planning the intervention.

5. Consider having a qualified interventionist act as an intermediary on your behalf.

CHAPTER FIVE

CARRYING OUT AN INTERVENTION

GROUP VERSUS PRIVATE INTERVENTIONS

Group interventions were first introduced during the 1960's in large part through the innovative work of the Reverend Vernon Johnson at the Johnson Institute in Minneapolis, Minnesota. Johnson was a recovering alcoholic who devoted himself to research on chemical dependency and developed the group intervention procedure as a way of overcoming the resistance of alcoholics to accepting treatment.

By reaching out to help other alcoholics through intervention, Johnson was essentially applying the last of the Twelve Steps of the Alcoholics Anonymous program, which dated back to the 1930's. Johnson and his colleagues were highly successful with group interventions that they personally organized and directed, proving beyond doubt that alcoholics can be effectively treated before they hit bottom with the more severe physical and mental disorders of late stage disease. During the 1980's, Johnson reported a success rate of 70% to 80% with patients referred to treatment.*

Shortly after my recovery in 1989, I studied at the Johnson Institute and incorporated Johnson's group model into my own intervention practice. But I later departed from that traditional approach by necessity when I was challenged by a group of clients in Chicago.

*Intervention: A Step-by-Step Guide for Families and Friends of Chemically Dependent Persons, Hazelden Foundation, Center City, MN, 1998 (previously published by the Johnson Institute, 1986), p. 9.

CASE NOTES: "GARBAGE HEAD"

After interviewing six family members, I quickly realized that they were all so hurt and angry that if I put them in the room with the drug user, they would most likely have lynched the fellow. So I had no choice but to meet with him privately. He was staying in a $20-a-night, fleabag motel, and I was forewarned by my clients that he was carrying a gun, which surprised me. Though many addicts do carry weapons, he was a scion of one of Chicago's most prominent families.

I called him early in the morning and let him know that his parents had asked me to talk with him. Without putting up too much resistance, he finally came out to meet me, and the first thing I did was to have him take his gun back to his room and leave it there. He turned out to be a decent enough young man, though sadly in the clutches of serious drug abuse. He used a little bit of everything, the type of addict known on the street as a "garbage head." He was desperate and in despair as many are. He also feared for his life. In so many words, he let me know that he was in trouble with some drug dealers.

We went into a coffee shop and talked for a couple hours. I already knew a great deal about his situation and had no trouble drawing him into conversation. In my pocket, I had written statements about his past that I had collected from each member of his family. By referring to these statements, I was able to confront him with the reality of his predicament, and he confided in ways that he never would have done in front of his family.

I have found when intervening that if I can get the alcoholic talking—if I can get the person to open up just the least little bit—he or she will usually do what I suggest. I listen carefully and never ask anyone point blank to go into treatment. I will map out a range of options that are available for two people sitting down to talk about a problem. In this instance, without ever resorting to threats or ultimatums, I was able to prevail upon him to go into a treatment center for 28 days as the best alternative that he had in his life at that moment.

The outcome was completely successful, and thus began my practice of private intervention, which I have refined over the years. Of course, not all interventions go that smoothly, especially when a family or group of friends tries to intervene on their own. If you intervene in this fashion and the meeting becomes hostile, you may suffer an onslaught of verbal abuse from the alcoholic and find the tables quickly turned on you. Here is a person whose opinion you may value more than anyone in the world suddenly telling you how everything is your fault and how despicable you are for having arranged this surprise party. Nothing is off-limits in these arguments, and this sort of intervention will frequently turn into rancorous quarreling with the group members ganging up on the alcoholic victim. Even if the encounter isn't violent but merely turns into a debate, you're in trouble. You may say something like, "Well, you did that," and the person says, "Oh, no, I didn't." Now you're in a spitting contest, the kind of verbal standoff that goes nowhere.

The reason that unguided interventions often degenerate in this way is because the participants are caught up in their own negative feelings. During the encounter they tend to forget in the heat of the moment that the addict is suffering from an illness. They fall back into the familiar defensive roles that they have been playing all along and end up attacking the person instead of the disease. This gives the alcoholic the opportunity to act out his or her negative emotions and once again to take refuge in denial. With his or her delusions still holding sway, the person will refuse to accept treatment, and afterwards, he or she is likely to flee to the nearest bar.

The professional interventionist has the advantage of objectivity by being outside the circle of family and friends who are personally involved with the alcoholic. Through interviews with the participants and counseling sessions, the interventionist can help determine the best way to proceed and guide the group, rehearsing its members prior to the intervention and anticipating the likely reactions that can be expected from the alcoholic. An experienced professional can also help the group members to recognize and to come to terms with their own defensive roles and negative feelings that have enabled the alcoholic to evade treatment in the past.

In my practice, I usually advise clients to take the safe road by allowing me to represent their interests through a private intervention during which I will meet alone with the afflicted person. When I go to that meeting, I always know that I have the group to fall back on for additional support in the rare instance when that might be necessary. But in most of my cases, I have been able to overcome the alcoholic's denials and defenses without having to involve the group directly. After persuading the alcoholic to accept an immediate course of clinical treatment, I continue to work with the person on a regular basis through the first year of his or her recovery, and nine out of ten times, the outcome is successful.

Depending on the situation, both the intermediary and group approaches to intervention have merit and are discussed below. You should weigh each option carefully to decide which is best for you. Whether a professional intervenes privately or with the group, the strategy and goals are the same; and either way, the ongoing support and input from the group are crucial. By confronting the alcoholic in a firm, caring manner with the evidence of his or her illness, the person can be compelled to face reality, and, once that happens, his or her resistance to treatment can be overcome.

RECRUITING THE INTERVENTION TEAM

In addition to your confidante, you will need other allies—ideally, a team of three to six people—to help you make the case to the alcoholic that he or she needs to accept help. Each of these team members should be someone who has a meaningful relationship with the afflicted person and has witnessed the person's behavior when he or she was drinking or using. The team should be made up only of individuals who can exert influence on the person and whose opinions he or she respects.

In making the case during the intervention, there can be strength in numbers, with each team member providing his or her firsthand knowledge of the person's drinking or using. You are likely to discover along the way that some team members know more about the extent of the problem than you do. The more testimony you have to present to the alcoholic about the reality of his or her condition, the more likely you are to be able to break through the person's rationalizations and delusions. The alcoholic's denials will collapse only when he or she is confronted with irrefutable evidence coming from a group that is motivated solely by shared concern and the desire to provide care.

As you prepare a list of potential team members, you might ask yourself a question that I often ask my clients: "If the person were to die tomorrow, who would be the six pall bearers at the funeral?"

Each of these hypothetical pall bearers should be considered as a possible participant in the intervention, with some important exceptions:

- Drinking buddies or fellow drug users.
- Emotionally unstable people

Drinking buddies and fellow drug users. Obviously, anyone who is chemically dependent should not be included on your list of possible candidates for the team. It may be that the person's social circle is comprised primarily of drinkers and users, in which case, you may need to turn to old friends who predate the person's descent into dependency. Or you may want to invite more distant family relations to take part, if possible. I have represented a number of clients on interventions that were essentially family reunions orchestrated across the country. In other cases, I have collected written testimony from family members who lived in different cities and then carried out the intervention without ever having the group assemble in one place.

Emotionally unstable individuals. Prospective team members should be ruled out if they lack the emotional stability or temperament to participate. This is especially true with the group approach, which requires all participants to confront the afflicted person directly rather than having a professional act on their behalf. *All participants must be prepared to conduct themselves in a responsible, non-antagonistic manner.* A group intervention should exclude anyone who might be too enraged to be able to control his or her anger toward the alcoholic. Similarly, anyone who might be too paralyzed by fear to be able to contribute to the process should not participate.

With the foregoing comments in mind, you should consider recruiting allies from the following categories:

1. Family members.
2. Friends and neighbors
3. Members of the clergy
4. Physicians and other professionals
5. Employers and co-workers

Family members. Family participants can include the spouse or significant other, parents, siblings, and children of the afflicted person. If you are not a close relative, members of his or her immediate family may be able to help you by suggesting other potential allies for the team. The voices of loved ones can be a powerful chorus that brings to bear strong influence and leverage on the alcoholic. In order to be effective, family members must first be willing to abandon the enabling roles that they have played in the past. They need to stop protecting, blaming and attacking. When they take stock in this way and act in concert during the intervention to encourage the person to accept treatment, their combined impact can be decisive.

Children are deeply affected by the alcoholic's behavior and are usually already aware that a problem exists. With professional guidance, even young children frequently take part in interventions. Children over the age of seven or eight who are able to verbalize their feelings can benefit from participating in the encounter by speaking out about their own experiences and learning about the disease. In many cases, the feelings of hurt and disappointment that they have been covering up can be aired safely for the first time. With the loving support of adults during the intervention, children can unburden themselves in this way and begin to redefine their relationships with the alcoholic in a positive way.

Of course, caution should be exercised with children when there is any possibility of violence or destructive behavior on the parts of either the alcoholic or the team members. In cases where the child is too young or confused to take part, I will have the sober parent write a letter to the alcoholic on behalf of the child. Such a letter may say something along the lines, "I love you, Daddy, but I don't want to grow up with a drunk for a father." Later, to underscore the point, I may ask the alcoholic if that is how he wants to be remembered by his children after he is gone.

Friends and neighbors. Participants outside the immediate family should be limited to those whose opinions carry weight with the afflicted person and those who can serve as credible witnesses to the person's past behavioral lapses. Non-family members often bring a valuable perspective to the intervention by being able to separate the person from the delusional syndrome that distorts reality within the family. For example, a husband might repeatedly blame his wife for his drinking or using, but a friend who has witnessed his behavior over time may be able to dispel that particular rationalization.

Members of the clergy. If the alcoholic attends a church or synagogue, then his or her priest, minister or rabbi might be invited to join the team, but only if he or she has firsthand knowledge of the person's condition or has some experience in counseling or treating alcohol and drug dependent persons.

Physicians and other professionals. The same considerations apply to doctors and therapists as apply to friends, clergy and other non-family members—they must have useful information to contribute about the alcoholic's condition and their opinions should be held in high regard by the afflicted person. Physicians and therapists should not be included if they have a professional bias or agenda that does not support the intervention.

Many physicians are not trained to deal with chemical dependency beyond the physical ailments caused by the illness, and many therapists underestimate or fail to diagnose the disease within the context of other mental disorders. On the other hand, there are doctors and therapists who have some experience with interventions and might serve as valuable members of your team. You will need to do some research into the backgrounds of such professionals and feel them out about their views regarding intervention and treatment.

Employers and co-workers. An employer can be a highly effective team member if he or she is already aware of the alcoholic's problem and willing to provide support in line with company policy. Employers and co-workers should not be approached if, as far as you know, they are not yet aware of the problem. As mentioned earlier, you may find yourself facing some legal liability if the alcoholic should lose his or her job because of your disclosures to the employer or co-workers. However, if you are an employer planning an intervention, you can use the afflicted person's job security as leverage to get the person into treatment, and the support of his or her family and friends can further strengthen your hand.

Each member of the team must be aware that the chemically dependent person is at a disadvantage suffering from an illness and each must be willing to put his or her relationship with the person on the line by taking part in the intervention. To meet these conditions, you may have to educate your allies with what you have learned about the disease. They need to understand that the illness is an involuntary condition, that the alcoholic's behavior is not deliberate. They should also realize that the alcoholic's delusions prevent him or her from recognizing the illness, that the person is unable to help himself or herself. Some members of the team may have to be won over by making them more aware of the extent and severity of the problem.

Before you start to contact the potential allies on your list, you should be prepared to meet with resistance from those who have reservations. Reluctance to become involved can take any number of forms. The alcoholic's spouse may not want to jeopardize the marriage. A child may be afraid of provoking the chemically dependent parent's anger. Others may not want to risk their friendships or professional relationships with the alcoholic. You will need to persuade those reluctant allies that there is no other way to deal with the problem, that the person's condition will only worsen unless he or she goes into treatment, that nothing less than his or her life is on the line. The bottom line argument with which you have convinced yourself of the necessity to intervene can be shared with those who you attempt to recruit: *Unless the person gets help, he or she will die prematurely.*

If you become frustrated with your efforts to build your team, you may want to turn to a professional to help make the case with reluctant participants. There may be team members who are willing to talk with you about the alcoholic's condition but are unwilling to face the person and offer their personal testimony in the setting of an intervention. In this situation, a professional can step in to act on behalf of the group and privately intervene with the alcoholic. Members of the group will be asked to supply their written testimony about the alcoholic's behavior in letter form for the interventionist, but in this way they can avoid any awkwardness or discomfort that they may feel about directly confronting the chemically dependent person.

FINDING A PROFESSIONAL INTERVENTIONIST

Qualified professionals are available in most parts of the country. The Resource Directory in the Appendix of this book will help you to locate counselors and interventionists in your area. Most reputable substance abuse and mental health treatment centers can offer you referrals. Additional resources can be obtained through a number of social agencies, including the Public Health Department and Department of Mental Health. The Substance Abuse and Mental Health Services Administration provides a valuable resource clearing house through its Office of Communications (contact the office by phone at 301-443-8956 or e-mail at info@samhsa.gov, or visit their Website at http://www.samhsa.gov/).

The cost of professional intervention can vary as much as the cost of services for doctors, therapists, and others in the medical field. Interventions are not usually covered by insurance, Medicaid, and Medicare. However, many interventionists are committed to providing quality care to all, and even those of us who charge many thousands of dollars will often work with you to find a way to make the services affordable. In addition, many local AA and Al-Anon groups can provide the names and telephone numbers of recovering alcoholics in the Twelve Step Program who offer private counseling and conduct interventions at no cost.

You are strongly advised to review the credentials and experience of any professional before retaining his or her services. You should interview the prospective interventionist by phone and/or face-to-face to find out that person's views on chemical dependency and treatment. The interventionist should welcome your questions, and you will want answers to the following:

- How many interventions has he or she conducted? What percentage of those interventions were successful in getting the alcoholic into treatment? How many of those patients are still in recovery after one year? Five years? Ten years?

- Is the interventionist a recovering alcoholic? What other experience has he or she had in working with chemically dependent persons?

- How long does the interventionist provide care after the alcoholic goes into treatment? Does he or she offer family and workplace counseling? Does the interventionist believe in treatment for the entire family through AA, NA, Al-Anon, Alateen, Cocaine Anonymous and similar Twelve Step groups?

- What reputable treatment centers offer referrals to the interventionist? Does he or she conduct private as well as group interventions?

FINDING A TREATMENT CENTER

You will need to make arrangements with a clinical treatment center in advance of the intervention. You should be prepared to get the chemically dependent person into treatment immediately. In my practice, I may give the person a choice between two treatment facilities, after having made prior, tentative arrangements with each to admit the person on the day of the intervention. The Substance Abuse and Mental Health Services Administration lists more than 11,000 treatment centers nationwide through its Office of Communications (see their Website listed above or call toll-free at 800-662-HELP for their treatment referral assistance).

The Yellow Pages provides listings under "Alcoholism Information and Treatment Centers" and "Mental Health Services." Many social agencies and local Twelve Step groups can also offer recommendations on treatment facilities. Employers can obtain information on Employee Assistance Programs from the Employee Assistance Professionals Association (contact their office at 703-387-1000 or visit the Web site at http://www.eap-association.com). Additional resources can be found through the National Institute of Alcohol Abuse and Alcoholism (NIAAA), a division of the Department of Health and Human Services (contact their office by phone at 301-443-3885 or visit their Website at http://www.niaaa.nih.gov/).

Once you have listings for treatment centers, contact them for further information. Ask for their brochures and publications. Find out about their short and long-term success rates, what types of insurance coverage they accept, whether or not they provide detoxification and aftercare programs, and whether or not they routinely work with any of the Twelve Step groups. You will also want to know if the treatment center supports the process of intervention.

If you have retained the services of a professional interventionist, he or she may make further recommendations about specific treatment centers as well as the possibility of outpatient versus inpatient care. Further discussion of treatment programs is provided in the next chapter.

COLLECTING WRITTEN STATEMENTS FROM THE GROUP

Each member of the group needs to write a statement offering eyewitness testimony about the alcoholic's actions and behavior under the influence. Written as a letter addressed to the alcoholic, each personal statement presents a list of incidents that came about because of the alcoholic's drinking or using. Rather than offering vague generalizations and personal opinions about the alcoholic, these letters should describe in detail specific events that have happened. Broad observations like "You're drinking too much" and stale pronouncements like "You have to quit drinking" are of no value and should be edited out of the letters. Statements that the alcoholic will interpret as personal attacks should also be avoided. Remarks like "You're nothing but a drunk" or "You're a junkie" serve no purpose whatsoever and are only likely to antagonize the afflicted person.

Each letter should be written in the personal style of the particular group member who is offering testimony. A letter can be as brief as a few paragraphs or might run several pages. The text should be organized roughly into three sections:

1. The opening section should express affection and concern for the alcoholic. The group member might want to refer to intimate or personal moments in his or her relationship with the alcoholic. The letter should also state at the beginning that the group member has become concerned because the person has a problem with alcohol or drugs.

2. The middle section should list and recount those specific events and incidents which the group member witnessed that have led him or her to believe the afflicted person has a problem. The letter should state exactly how the group member felt about each incident.

3. The concluding section should pose the question of whether or not the person will accept the help that has been arranged by the group. The question should be

phrased to elicit a yes or no response. "Will you accept our help and agree to go into treatment today?" The group member may also include an ultimatum demanding that the person enter treatment.

The letter might take the following form as a guideline in the case of a wife writing to her afflicted husband:

Dear Harry,

First, I want you to know I love you very much. I always have and always will. That is why this is so difficult for me. INCLUDE POSITIVE POINTS ABOUT THE PERSON. You were always so intelligent and funny. It was such a pleasure just to be with you. RECALL A SPECIFIC INCIDENT THAT WAS A POSITIVE SHARED EXPERIENCE. I remember when we first met....I remember how you were on our honeymoon....etc. EXPRESS YOUR CONCERN. Sadly, times have changed and you have changed, and I have come to understand that alcohol (or drugs) are responsible. I have seen what drinking (or using) has done to you, to me and to us. I have become more and more upset and concerned about you.

LIST ONE OR MORE SPECIFIC INCIDENTS DURING WHICH ALCOHOL OR DRUGS CAUSED AN UNPLEASANT, DANGEROUS OR EMBARRASSING SITUATION. PROVIDE DETAILS INCLUDING TIME, PLACE AND OTHER PEOPLE WHO WERE INVOLVED. On Christmas Eve, you were late coming home and you were so drunk that you stumbled into the Christmas tree and knocked it over. Last Thursday morning I had to call your boss and cover up for you because *you were in bed with a hangover. The night before you vomited on the bathroom floor and passed out...etc.* DESCRIBE HOW EACH OF THESE EVENTS MADE YOU FEEL. *I was hurt and infuriated by your behavior that night...etc.*

EXPLAIN WHAT YOU HAVE LEARNED ABOUT CHEMICAL DEPENDENCY. *Harry, because you are so important to me and I want our marriage to survive, I have taken the time to learn about alcohol and drug problems. I have learned that you are unable to recognize the seriousness of the problem, but that it can be treated successfully. Most importantly, I have learned that you can't deal with the problem alone, and that is why I am here to offer my love and support as you face this challenge. I am committed to stand by you every step of the way.*

REVEAL THE ARRANGEMENTS THAT YOU HAVE MADE FOR IMMEDIATE TREATMENT. *I have done some research and reserved a place for you at a treatment center that comes highly recommended.* GIVE THE NAME AND LOCATION OF THE FACILITY. *The program is short-term and designed to give you the chance to learn about the problem and to live your life without alcohol (or drugs). Harry, I am asking you to accept my love and support and to take this opportunity to put the problem behind you.*

ISSUE AN APPROPRIATE ULTIMATUM THAT PLACES THE FUTURE OF THE RELATIONSHIP ON THE LINE. *If you choose not to accept my help, then it is clear that you are choosing alcohol (or drugs) over anything I ever meant to you or anything you ever meant to yourself. If you reject this opportunity, then I am prepared to leave you*

---

and will file for divorce, if necessary. I hope you will make the right choice, but ultimately the choice is yours.

POSE THE CRUCIAL QUESTION. *Harry, please take this first step right now and the rest will follow. Will you accept this offer of help and go into treatment?*

Such letters will be used in a number of ways depending on the type of intervention. As we will see, in a group intervention, the letters will serve as scripts to be read aloud to the alcoholic in the presence of the team. In a private intervention, the content of the letters may be referred to as evidence by the interventionist without being read. Or, if necessary to make the case more compelling during the encounter, the interventionist may read one or more of the letters to the chemically dependent person. After the alcoholic goes into treatment, the letters will be given to his or her treatment counselors to inform them about the person's background and the specific symptoms of his or her illness. The letters also may be used to advantage in group therapy and private counseling sessions.

REHEARSING THE GROUP INTERVENTION

You will need to have one or two rehearsals of the group to prepare for the intervention and to avoid any conflicts that might otherwise occur. These practice sessions are routinely conducted under the guidance of the professional interventionist and should include all of the participants except for the chemically dependent person.

REHEARSALS CAN ACCOMPLISH THE FOLLOWING:

1. The group can be further educated about the nature of the illness.

2. Members of the group can work through their negative feelings with each other and the interventionist to reduce the likelihood of antagonism during the intervention.

3. The group's shared goals can be affirmed in an atmosphere of mutual support.

4. The group's letters can be reviewed and edited to avoid any inappropriate or inflammatory remarks. The interventionist can coach each participant about what to say and what not to say during the intervention.

5. Likely reactions of the chemically dependent person can be anticipated and an appropriate group response to each can be prepared.

6. The rehearsals allow the group to foresee potential problems and can give participants the opportunity at the eleventh hour to change course by having the interventionist act privately on their behalf with the chemically dependent person.

During rehearsals, questions should be encouraged and information shared among the participants. They should first discuss and review the characteristic emotional and delusional syndromes of the disease. Once the group reaches a shared understanding of the illness and how it affects the chemically dependent person, the participants can proceed with planning the practical details of the intervention and with rehearsing the group. Each decision along the way requires a consensus among the members. The group should be in agreement on exactly how, when and where the intervention will take place.

The steps are as follows:

1. Appoint a chairperson.

2. Read through the written statements.
3. Anticipate the reactions of the chemically dependent person.
4. Determine the specific kind of leverage that each participant will bring to bear.
5. Decide where and when the intervention will take place.

Appoint a chairperson. The first order of business will be to select a chairperson to direct the intervention and rehearsals. In many cases, the interventionist will take the initiative and assume this responsibility. He or she has the advantage of being outside the immediate family and can often help to avoid family quarrels. Sometimes a group member other than the professional can be more effective serving as chairperson because of the respect he or she commands with the alcoholic. For example, in a workplace intervention, the employer or supervisor may be able to step into the lead role and take advantage of his or her managerial skills and position of power on the job. Family members are often not suited for chairing the intervention because they harbor too many negative feelings toward the alcoholic and are likely to resort to spontaneous attacks during the encounter.

The authority of the chairperson to direct the intervention should be acknowledged by all participants. He or she can help determine the order for people to speak during the intervention, starting with those in the group who are most influential and closest to the chemically dependent person. The chairperson will also mediate and attempt to defuse any disputes that may arise between the group and the alcoholic. If the chairperson asks a group member to stop speaking at any point, he or she should be willing to follow the chairperson's direction and allow someone else to talk. The initial goal of the intervention is to have the alcoholic listen to the testimony offered by each of the participants as each reads his or her prepared statement. In line with this, the chairperson will need to use discretion to maintain order at the meeting and allow each member of the group to be heard in turn.

The chairperson will start the intervention with an introductory statement similar to what might be heard at the beginning of any formal meeting, but directed to the afflicted person. The statement should express concern for the person and explain the reason for the meeting, addressing him or her in a straightforward manner. "Because all of us are concerned about you, we are here to talk about your problem with alcohol and drugs. Each of us has something to say to you. This isn't going to be easy for you or for us. You will be given the chance to speak, but we ask that you listen to us first. Will you do that?" Note that the introductory statement clearly puts the alcoholic in the position of having to listen.

If the chairperson is a friend, employer or family member, he or she should introduce the professional interventionist. If I were being introduced in this capacity, the chairperson might say to the alcoholic, "You know everyone here except Bruce Cotter. We have invited Mr. Cotter because he is a consultant who helps families like ours with a loved one who has the kind of problem you have." I am often introduced to the afflicted person in similar fashion when I conduct private interventions. In such cases, after the introduction is made, I will ask to be left alone with the person in order to talk privately.

Read through the written statements. During the rehearsals, each member of the group should read his or her letter aloud to the others. The team should review each factual item listed in each letter. Remember that these written statements should voice concern and contain only descriptions of incidents—only those facts that will conclusively expose the alcoholic's behavior under the influence.

As the statements are read, others in the group can make suggestions about wording and content, removing anything in the statements that might be construed as hostile or antagonistic by the alcoholic. As discussed earlier, the tone of the letters should be one of sincere concern and good will. Name-calling must be eliminated. Likewise, generalizations and personal opinions condemning the afflicted person should be omitted. Any comment that might be interpreted as a personal attack can turn the intervention into an ugly squabble and sabotage the effort of the group.

As the letters are read, it is common for participants to make unexpected discoveries by sharing what they know with each other. In the past, the alcoholic's behavior may not have been discussed even though it was witnessed by all who are taking part in the intervention. When the silence is finally broken during the rehearsals, one or more group members are likely to say, "How did you know that? I thought that I was the only one who knew!" With the secrets of the alcoholic's behavior no longer being kept under wraps by the group, the person is likely to be vulnerable and that much more receptive to the prospect of going into treatment.

Anticipate the reactions of the chemically dependent person. During each rehearsal, the group members should try to characterize the probable response of the alcoholic as each statement is read. Participants should try to imagine the most likely excuses, denials and objections that the alcoholic might offer during the actual intervention. What will the person say and how will he or she act when confronted by the group?

You can bet that the alcoholic will put up a fight, and you need to be prepared to overcome his or her resistance. The

99

participants can decide beforehand how to respond to the person in such a way that his or her defenses can be defeated. The group has the advantage of knowing the facts and being able to present the reality of the situation item by item as the written statements are read aloud. Of course, the alcoholic's moment-by-moment responses cannot be entirely predicted, but you and your allies should be able to envision the probable range and tenor of the person's reactions.

It is sometimes helpful in rehearsals for one or more of the participants to take the part of the afflicted person and verbalize his or her likely responses to the group. The person may have said something in the past that can be quoted to give an indication of his or her usual sort of denial. A wife, for instance, may recall her husband's actual words when she confronted him about his drinking or using. He may have said, "What are you talking about? I don't have any problem except you nagging me! That's the only reason I drink." If the husband interrupts his wife with this sort of objection while she tries to read her statement, she will need to keep her calm and ask him to allow her to continue speaking. If the husband should threaten to walk out of the intervention, the chairperson or someone else may have to prevail upon him to stay in the room and listen. At all times during the intervention, the group members should be working together to find ways to compel the alcoholic to listen.

As you conduct your rehearsals and finalize your plans for the intervention, there is a common reaction by the alcoholic for which you should be prepared. When confronted with the evidence of his or her condition, the person may express remorse and anguish, and then cave in and tearfully promise to stop drinking and using forever. The person might be absolutely sincere and volunteer to attend AA meetings or enter outpatient care. But you have heard these promises before, and the group should be resolute about not giving in to any sort of compromise.

The person may insist that clinical treatment is unnecessary because he or she has now "seen the light" and is committed to reform. In this situation, at the very least, the person must agree to enter a treatment center at the first and slightest lapse. In my practice, I usually don't allow such a compromise to occur. When confronted with this kind of reluctance by the alcoholic, I explain to the person why it makes more sense to take care of the problem now, once and for all, and why, without immediate treatment, he or she will inevitably return to drinking and using.

We alcoholics have all tried to quit before. But we are rarely ever successful at following through on our vows of abstinence when we rely on our own effort as a sheer act of willpower. The alcoholic who attempts to stay sober in this way is referred to as a "dry drunk." The person may remain abstinent over an extended period of time, but he or she has not begun to deal with the illness and its mental symptoms. The emotional, spiritual and social aspects of the disease remain in force even though the person is not drinking or using.

During a period of self-imposed abstinence, the alcoholic is likely to be extremely anxious and irritable, frequently overreacting to any stress or frustration that comes along. What the person fails to realize is that, in the long run, sobriety involves much more than not drinking or using. Without alcohol or drugs, the person's life will become a painful vacuum, and that personal void can only be filled through a comprehensive program of treatment and recovery that addresses every aspect of the alcoholic's life.

Determine the specific kind of leverage that each

participant will bring to bear. During the rehearsals, the group can review the statements of each of those group members who present an individual ultimatum, which is an "or else" type of demand related to the alcoholic accepting immediate treatment. Each participant has to decide exactly what he or she is actually prepared to do if the alcoholic should refuse to accept help. Each group member should be asked, "What actions are you willing to take to get this person to accept treatment? What are you actually willing to do at this point? Will you put your relationship with the person on the line?" The ultimatums and specific leverage will vary from person to person depending on his or her relationship with the alcoholic.

As there is always a chance that the alcoholic will refuse treatment, *you should be prepared to follow through with whatever ultimatum you present.* In many cases, participants have made threats in the past and subsequently backed down from them. A husband or wife might have told the spouse any number of times, "If you don't stop drinking, I'm going to leave you." A teenage son or daughter may have said to a parent, "If you don't quit, I'm moving out of the house." An employer may have already threatened to fire the alcoholic without following through, or a friend may have threatened to end the relationship without doing so. Such hollow threats must now be replaced by serious promises that each participant is prepared to keep if necessary. If a wife is not really willing to leave her husband, she should not say that she is. Everything communicated to the alcoholic during the intervention must be realistic and honest.

Because, in many cases, the alcoholic has heard the threats before and knows that they were not carried out, the person will figure that somehow he or she will be able to get off the hook again. But by presenting the ultimatum in the formal setting of the intervention and by having unanimous group support, the person is now more likely to take the threat seriously. The alcoholic has to be made to realize that the party is now over, that this is crunch-time. When confronted in a firm, no-nonsense manner, he or she can be made aware for the first time that there will be unpleasant consequences if the drinking or using continues. Ultimately, the person must be made to realize, despite all of his or her objections, that there is no alternative other than going into treatment. At the point when that realization takes place, you will need to be ready to transport the person directly to the treatment center where you have arranged in advance for his or her admittance.

Decide where and when the intervention will take place. Ideally, with either a group or private intervention, the encounter should take place on neutral territory at a time when the chemically dependent person is not likely to be under the influence. Set the earliest date possible, and use whatever pretext is necessary to make sure the person attends the meeting. He or she may not expect you or others to be present, but the person will be made aware of the purpose of the encounter at the outset of the encounter, and the element of surprise will work in your favor.

The intervention should not be carried out in a public place like a restaurant where there are likely to be interruptions, noise and other distractions. It should be a place where both the alcoholic and the group can feel secure (private). I often use a conference room in a hotel, with the family stationed nearby to say their goodbyes before the person leaves for the treatment center. I usually try not to intervene in the person's home because he or she can simply ask me to leave or might threaten to call the police.

Another reason to avoid the home is that the alcoholic

may keep a weapon there. Others who know the person may be shocked to find out that he or she has a gun, but in our society this frequently turns out to be the case, even with the most pacific and unlikely people. Obviously, there is no place for a weapon in the emotionally volatile atmosphere of an intervention. In all cases where a violent reaction can be expected on the part of the alcoholic, the intervention should be handled privately by a qualified professional.

THE TYPICAL INTERVENTION SCENARIO

There are usually three distinct stages of the intervention. After the alcoholic starts to listen to the testimony of the group, the person is likely to feel the painful reality of his or her condition. At some point during this first stage, reality will break through and force the person to react without the armor of his or her defenses. The person may express shock, sorrow and embarrassment, often before all of the group members have finished reading their statements. Such a moment of truth can be quite dramatic, but the intervention is still far from over. With the person in that vulnerable state, he or she must listen to the rest of the testimony and be convinced to accept treatment without delay.

This second part of the intervention—compelling the person to accept immediate treatment—can be facilitated by having one or more members of the group present your demands and several treatment options. Describe the particular hospitals and clinics with which you have made arrangements. Your research into the programs offered by various treatment facilities will pay off at this point, and the person will feel like he or she has some choice in the matter. By letting the alcoholic take part in this decision, the person will be allowed to retain some sense of dignity.

Interventions are deeply emotional experiences for all who participate. Once the person agrees to accept help, the atmosphere is often one of great relief and shared optimism. With the decision to accept treatment, hope can now replace despair, and the event is often accompanied by a spontaneous outpouring of love. With some interventions, however, one or more of the participants may experience a letdown after the person leaves for treatment. There may be apprehension about what will happen next. Whatever the mood of the group may be after the person's departure, it is advisable to give everyone the opportunity to talk about their feelings. How does each person now feel about the intervention process and its resolution?

This third and final stage of the intervention allows for a shared sense of closure, but it also marks the beginning of a new set of challenges. You and your allies need to consider the kind of support that you will provide during the treatment period immediately ahead and the future tasks associated with long-term, continuing care. Life is not going to be the same after the person is released from treatment and returns home. You and your group need to be ready for the changes that lie ahead. These areas of concern will be discussed at length in the remaining chapters.

CONDUCTING THE INTERVENTION

After one or two rehearsals, you will be as prepared as you can be to follow through and carry out the intervention. The sense of urgency that you share with the group should allow you to overcome any remaining fears and uncertainties. There is no reason to prolong the rehearsal period. Even if you were to go through a hundred rehearsals, no one would be able to tell you exactly what will happen during the intervention.

Each situation is unique and depends on a large number of factors, all of which can vary a great deal: the personality of the alcoholic, the stage of his or her disease, the relationships of the group members to the alcoholic, the personalities and dynamics of the group, the kind of leverage that the group brings to bear on the alcoholic, and so forth.

By their very nature, interventions create anxiety for the participants. There is usually a stressful sense of anticipation. After all, the intervention is a confrontation, albeit one that is intended to be loving and constructive. The encounter itself is likely to be contentious and, therefore, is ultimately unpredictable. But if you have been conscientious and thorough with your planning, you have every reason to expect a positive outcome. You should be pleased with yourself for caring enough to wage this kind of noble effort. The intervention scenario is one where the logic of "right is might" applies in all cases, and you are unquestionably in the right. When the moment of truth arrives, you and your allies should feel empowered by your affection for the person and the practical knowledge that you have now accumulated about the illness.

Whenever I conduct an intervention, either privately or with a group, I truly believe that I am going to succeed in overcoming the alcoholic's resistance. In most cases, I am able to prevail upon the person to accept treatment without ever raising my voice or being drawn into heated arguments. The caring tone and personal dynamic that I bring to the conversation are crucial in getting the person not just to listen, but to hear and take to heart what I have to say. In this regard, my experience over the years dealing with alcoholics and their families may help you to avoid some common pitfalls.

When I begin a case, I am initially intent upon getting a grasp of the situation by collecting testimony from each member of the group, both in the form of written statements and through interviews with the participants. Many times I will be the first person with whom they are able to open up about the problem. They may have told others pieces of the story, but I am the first to hear the whole saga. This can be a healthy purging for those close to the alcoholic and usually requires one or more hours of conversation. They will tell me about the violence and abuse, the vomiting and blackouts. They will tell me about their loneliness and their sex lives or lack thereof, every intimate detail as it relates to the alcoholic's problem. All of this information can be extremely useful, and I encourage my clients to leave nothing out.

As the group presents the testimony, I am constantly scanning the evidence about the person's condition and looking for the appropriate hook that I can use as effective leverage to get the alcoholic to make the right choice. What does this person care about deeply enough to cause him or her to face the problem? What is the fallout in the home and at the workplace? What has happened because of the drinking or using? Where and when did the incidents take place? Give me the specifics:

Lately, she gets drunk by six o'clock and then passes out after dinner. He is not showing up for meetings, not coming home for days at a time. She embarrassed me in front of our friends. He was arrested for a DWI and slapped me around when I tried to talk about the problem.

Not all of the testimony is dramatic, but as I talk to two or three people and collect their written statements, I get an overall picture of the situation. I will have that evidence in my pocket when I meet the alcoholic. The written testimony is my trump card, but more often than not I don't even have to read the statements to the alcoholic. If he or she insists, "I don't have a problem," I will then make use of the testimony. I may say, "I met with your family, and they believe that you have a problem with alcohol. But I want to hear your side of the story. Is your family overreacting?" My tone is never accusatory, but simply communicates my interest in discussing what I have been told and my desire to help. I may put it more bluntly, "Either we have six people who are lying to me about you, or you're lying to me about you." Invariably, the alcoholic will try to minimize or deny the problem, but I have a pocketful of incriminating pieces of evidence that I can use as needed.

I try to be sensitive to the feelings and defenses that come into play with those close to the afflicted person, especially with family members. *I am always on the lookout for anyone who is so filled with hostility that his or her participation in the group will jeopardize the procedure.* I will not allow such a person to be present during the intervention. When dealing with family members who have suffered a great deal of emotional pain as a result of the alcoholic's behavior, I advise them to undergo professional counseling and join one of the family support groups such as Al-Anon.

Because in many cases the problem has been festering for years, family members are vulnerable to their own rationalizations and delusions. They can be as out of touch with reality as the alcoholic and equally resistant to accepting help. They will need to be persuaded down the line, but my immediate concern is guiding the chemically dependent person through the intervention. My overriding goal is to get the person away from drugs and alcohol and into a safe environment. I cannot allow the needs of the family, as pressing as those needs may be, to get in the way of that primary objective, and neither should you.

Private intervention is usually the preferable approach when the alcoholic is a husband or wife and the non-drinking spouse is locked into feelings of animosity and self-pity. When the spouse engages in a habitual pattern of enabling over a long period of time, the situation is sometimes described as one of "codependency." The couple is likely to be drawn into the same destructive scenes over and over, with each partner feeding the other's hostilities and delusions. In this type of case, the non-drinking spouse is so deeply immersed in protecting, blaming and attacking that he or she is essentially suffering from the same illness. But the alcoholic's problem with chemical abuse is still more urgent and must be addressed first. Only after intervening with the alcoholic husband or wife and getting that person into treatment can I turn my attention to the spouse.

CASE NOTES: THE HUNT CLUB

After intervening and admitting one alcoholic husband into a treatment center, his wife told me in all seriousness, "Our weekly cocktail parties at the Hunt Club are a vital part of our lives and marriage. So, make sure all of this intervention business doesn't screw that up." Initially, I humored her by saying that I would alert the treatment team to give him just enough sobriety to allow him to continue to get drunk at the Hunt Club but nowhere else. Obviously, that was a case where both spouses were in urgent need of treatment and counseling.

Prior to every intervention, I remind myself never to underestimate the disease. When I confront the chemically dependent person, I know that I am facing the kind of desperate opponent who will fight dirty, tooth and nail, and do everything possible to frustrate my efforts. It's a kind of psychological brawl, and I'm prepared for the worst because I realize that addiction brings out the worst kind of behavior in people. Because the addict is sick, I know better than to take personally anything that he or she may say to me. There is nothing fair about this disease and the way that it controls its victims, and therefore, I use whatever means may be necessary to carry the day.

When I walk into the room to meet with the alcoholic for the first time, I have the advantage of knowing that the person is not getting the pleasure from drinking or using that he or she derived in the past. Whatever the person's attitude and outward demeanor may be when we meet, I know that he or she is actually in pain because I have been there myself and have seen it so many times. Many alcoholics seem to wear their frayed nerves several inches above their skin. Many are on the edge of despair and quite fragile, and as such, I approach the person with a velvet glove. I always make it clear that I am there only to help and to act in his or her best interests.

Though I am firm and clearly on the offensive, I am not trying to intimidate or beat up the person emotionally. I weigh my words carefully. At first, I don't know which words will work in my favor, and above all, which will hurt the person. Many with the disease have been treated like second-class citizens for so long that they appreciate the attention and just want to talk. I explain up front that I will keep everything that we discuss in complete confidence. I avoid using words like "addict" and "alcoholic." Nor do I refer to the "disease" but only to the "problem" that the individual has with alcohol or drugs. The person will have to reach his or her own conclusions about the illness through the process of treatment and recovery.

INTERVENING WITH ADOLESCENTS AND SENIOR CITIZENS

Adolescent and elderly alcoholics pose special challenges when it comes to both intervention and treatment. Young people often lose their way with alcohol or drugs before they have a strong sense of identity and direction in life. They may find themselves in conflict with their parents and rebel against authority at home and in school. I will tell a teenage addict, "If you try going straight, you have a chance in this world. If you don't try, you have no chance. Why not give it a shot?" Teens will often say to me, "I'd rather die!" But they don't really mean that, and I will usually challenge them to explain the situation. My willingness to listen to their gripes and complaints lets them know that I care, even if no one else does. They may lie to me 90% of the time, but 10% of what they say will be valuable later in treatment. Young adults are most likely to commit themselves to recovery when their parents educate themselves about the disease and provide ongoing support.

Older people often fall victim to alcohol and drugs when retirement causes them to lose direction in life. You may have an aggressive businessman who takes retirement at fifty-five or sixty. The fellow moves to a retirement community and joins a country club, but at this point he has nothing meaningful to do with his life. He doesn't know how to deal with his newfound leisure, and everywhere he goes someone hands him a screwdriver. How much time can he fill with bridge and golf? He may have been a social drinker in the past, but his life is now an endless cocktail party. After an intervention pulls him back from the brink, this type of person will often approach treatment with the same kind of all-out commitment that he previously brought into his work life. With support from family and friends, his chances for full recovery are excellent.

No one is ever too old to benefit from treatment. Only a year after I intervened with one elderly patient, I learned that she had subsequently died of cancer. Her daughter wrote me a letter:

CASE NOTES: A GRATEFUL DAUGHTER

"Mom was diagnosed with lung cancer and died in October, 2001. She was an amazing woman and stepped up to the plate when challenged. When she was diagnosed, she was able to deal with the physical and emotional aspects of cancer because of her experience being treated for alcoholism. God works in mysterious ways. He led us to you to help prepare for the road ahead of us. I learned to love and respect my mother for the many beautiful traits that she had. I was given a bonus year with her that I would not trade for the world. The last year of her life was completely different than it would have been if she had still been drinking."

Many of those I see in my practice have been through treatment before. When they come to me, I'm often the last resort for their families. I may surprise an elderly husband by saying, "Your wife tells me that you were in treatment two years ago. What went wrong there? Why didn't things work out for you?" He might complain about having been in a facility where he was surrounded by younger patients with whom he had little in common. He may say, "Look, I'm sixty years old and I was with teenagers, kids who were wearing their baseball caps backwards. I couldn't stand their music and foul language. I felt old." I will turn this around by assuring him,

"I can understand why you felt out of place there, but I know of several clinics that would be ideal for you."

There are a growing number of treatment facilities around the country that provide separate accommodations and counseling programs that are tailored to meet the needs of patients in the upper and lower age brackets. If the afflicted person in your life is an adolescent or a senior, you will want to investigate this type of specialized treatment option. More information on these programs can be obtained from treatment centers and through the resources listed in the Appendix.

WHAT IF THE INTERVENTION FAILS?

In a sense, no intervention ever fails even if the chemically dependent person refuses to accept treatment. Even in that worst-case scenario, the person's awareness of the problem has changed dramatically and the idea of treatment as a viable option has been placed on the table. I have intervened with many alcoholics who initially refused to accept help but changed their minds within a matter of days or weeks. If you are frustrated by your first attempt to intervene, the best advice that anyone can give you is to try again as many times as necessary. You have already rallied support for the cause, and the alcoholic has been given notice in no uncertain terms. You have seen the person's reactions and are now in a position to press your advantage.

When properly conducted, *virtually all interventions set positive changes into motion.* Those who participate are no longer isolated and powerless. They have been educated about the disease and no longer have to blame themselves or the alcoholic for the problem. Those in the family who discover that they need help can reach out to others for assistance. Most importantly, the group has come between the alcoholic and his or her drug of choice. In the future, that person will find it difficult, if not impossible, to resort to the same rationalizations and denials. Both the alcoholic and his or her family now have the chance to work toward recovery where before the situation was hopeless.

CHAPTER FIVE
SUMMARY POINTS

**Both private and group
interventions must be planned in advance.
A checklist of tasks should include the following:**

1. Recruit allies for the intervention team.

2. Recruit a professional interventionist and decide on a group or private approach.

3. Research treatment centers and select two or more viable options.

4. Collect written testimony from the group members in the form of letters to the chemically dependent person.

5. Conduct one or two rehearsals to prepare for the intervention.

6. Choose a chairperson to direct rehearsals and lead the intervention.

7. Read and edit the team's written testimony during rehearsals.

8. Decide on the type of leverage and specific ultimatum that each group member will bring to bear.

9. Anticipate the person's likely reactions to the written testimony. Plan the group's responses to the person's objections.

10. Decide on a time and place to conduct the intervention. Arrange in advance for the person to be admitted to one or more treatment centers on the day of the intervention.

CHAPTER SIX

SUPPORTING THE ALCOHOLIC DURING TREATMENT

Entering Clinical Treatment

After the intervention, the chemically dependent person should be transported to the treatment facility directly and without delay. This is a crucial time because, prior to admission, the patient is likely to experience anxiety and have second thoughts about the decision to enter treatment. The person will have time during the trip to consider the fact that he or she is now facing a month or more of complete abstinence. Admission to the treatment center is voluntary, and the prospect of being cut off from the drug is deeply unsettling and often terrifying for the alcoholic, since the person still perceives the chemical as his or her god. Some alcoholics become quiet and passive before admission, resigning themselves to get through the treatment period by acquiescing and simply blending into the wallpaper, while secretly planning to return to using after release. They intend to beat the system any way they can, but such ruses will be uncovered soon enough and addressed in therapy.

While en route to the treatment center, many patients voice last minute misgivings, and you should be prepared to offer both reassurance and firm insistence if you meet with any waffling along the way. I've heard all kinds of excuses for delaying entering treatment.

117

CASE NOTES: "NOT TODAY BECAUSE..."

. . . I have a manicure on Thursday.

. . . I have to finalize the deal on an international merger next Tuesday.

. . . The pool man is finally coming tomorrow.

. . . I need more time to pack. What will the weather be like? Do we dress for dinner?

. . . My son's Bar Mitzvah is at the end of the month.

. . . I've waited three months to get a haircut appointment with Xavier!

In reality, when setting the date for the intervention, with the family or employer, any upcoming event of significance has already been considered. Rather than putting yourself in this position, you can have the professional interventionist assume responsibility for transporting the person to the clinic or hospital.

Some treatment centers offer only primary care on site and have their patients admitted to a detoxification unit at an outside general hospital. In many cases, the professional will have an ongoing relationship with the treatment facility and can help expedite the admissions process.

When I accompany an alcoholic to a treatment center, I always stay with the person while he or she is being admitted. Upon arrival, we will be met by a case manager who will interview the patient and guide him or her through the admissions procedure. It is in everyone's best interest to have the admission run as smoothly and quickly as possible. The patient will be asked to sign a permission form acknowledging his or her agreement to accept medical treatment. While the terms of payment must be arranged in advance, there may be insurance and other financial forms to be filled out.

Once the necessary paperwork is completed, the patient will be given a thorough medical examination and then placed in a detoxification unit for 48 to 72 hours. After being assigned a bed, the patient is kept under observation and closely monitored while he or she withdraws from the toxic effects of the drug. This period of detox and observation may need to be extended when there is any risk of suicide or seizures due to withdrawal. Many patients go into detox and sleep a great deal for those first few days. They are often disoriented and may remain in a kind of mental fog during the first couple of weeks of treatment.

After the initial detox period, the patient will be transferred to primary care and assigned a counselor. That primary counselor will consult with the interventionist and the family to find out about the patient's background, home and work situations. The counselor will also create a profile of the person's alcohol and drug use. In my practice with patients entering treatment, I arrange for the counselor to speak with family members as soon as possible. I also provide the counselor with the written statements that were collected prior to the intervention. Giving the counselor a complete rundown on the patient saves precious time and prevents the patient from misleading the treatment staff about his or her situation.

Patients typically bring their delusions, denials and rationalizations into therapy, attempting to wield them as defensive weapons just as they have been all along. They will try to hide their identities and express indignant outrage about how they are being mistreated. When I went into treatment, I was so sick and evasive that I had the staff believing I was working at the time in Washington D.C. as a top media consultant, which was actually the kind of career position that I had lost a number of times because of my drinking. The counselors were taken in by my deceit for a couple of weeks until they were able to ferret out the truth, that I had been unemployed for more than a year and had a long history of alcohol-related problems.

After entering treatment, alcoholics will concoct every imaginable fabrication to conceal or minimize the illness. Afflicted husbands often claim, "My wife is the one who is the alcoholic, but she tricked me into coming here. I don't have a problem." That type of denial is common and needs to be challenged with evidence from the family and others who participated in the intervention. The patient's denials waste valuable time. Every minute is critical when counselors are working under a 28-day time limit. Many patients have been drinking or using for years, and a month of treatment is barely enough time to address the problem and initiate the recovery process.

After the patient is moved to primary care, he or she will attend both lectures and counseling sessions aimed at educating the person about the disease, and about himself or herself.

Case Notes: The Wall Street Broker

Often a patient will spend the first week or two in treatment complaining, and just figuring how to go through the motions until they can be "sprung." In this case the patient, a type-A Wall Street broker, complained and moaned, and displayed a condescending attitude toward every aspect of his proposed recovery. However, when I went to see him for his mid-treatment visit, I noticed a real change in his attitude. He was more reserved and seemed more at peace. When I asked him about it, he said, "I just realized I have a disease and I'm not the rat I thought I was. It just dawned on me that these lectures are about me.

I just thought they were talking about the losers and nuts all around me."

Self-examination is an essential aspect of the treatment process, accomplished through individual psychiatric counseling, group encounters with other patients, and often through AA and related Twelve Step meetings. The patient is given a crash course designed to enable him or her to recognize the illness and understand the life-or-death gravity of the problem. Through education and interactions with the clinical staff and other patients, the alcoholic's defenses can be overcome on a daily basis. Rather than taking an adversarial approach, most treatment programs operate on a strategy of positive reinforcement and constructive criticism. Instead of attacking and blaming the patient, counselors and therapists will emphasize those personal qualities and goals that deserve praise and encouragement, working consistently to remedy the alcoholic's shattered self-esteem.

Group sessions can be confrontational, disconcerting and painful at times, as both staff and fellow patients point out the alcoholic's defensive rationalizations. But with a growing awareness of the illness as it relates to his or her personal history, the patient can begin to take responsibility for past behavior and develop a positive outlook, instilled with a belief that his or her life can change for the better. A successful course of treatment is one in which the patient is discharged with hope for the future balanced by the knowledge that he or she has a chronic, progressive illness for which sobriety is the only remedy.

WHAT TO EXPECT WHILE THE ALCOHOLIC IS IN TREATMENT

I advise my clients not to visit or call the patient for at

least two weeks after the patient is admitted into treatment. This is especially important for family members. Often after a patient goes through several days of detoxification, he or she will feel better and decide that the treatment has already brought about a miracle cure. The person will claim to have seen the light and may decide to check out of the center against medical advice. In many cases, the patient will turn to the family and to those who intervened in order to win their support for his or her decision to withdraw from treatment. This can become yet another desperate con game, with the alcoholic resorting once again to manipulation and emotional blackmail.

CASE NOTES: "HELP! THEY'RE TORTURING ME!"

I had a case where a wealthy socialite claimed that she had been assigned a roommate who was a crack-addicted prostitute. That was, in fact, not the case, but her family believed her and promptly dispatched a private jet to bring her home. Other patients have played for sympathy from their loved ones by insisting that they are being beaten or tied to their beds.

In cases where the husband or wife has been drinking for ten or fifteen years, the non-drinking spouse will have a long history of hollow threats. "If you don't stop drinking, I'm going to leave you," or "If you don't quit, I'm going to throw you out." If the alcoholic has seen the spouse repeatedly back down from such threats, he or she will expect the same thing to happen again. After entering treatment, the patient will assume that he or she can go home simply by refining the sales pitch. "I've been in treatment for two days, and now I really understand the problem. I'm ready to come home. I can really do this the right way now."

Families and friends should be prepared to encounter every type of argument, as many alcoholics are insidiously clever at making the case for early discharge. As there is always the possibility that those close to the alcoholic will cave in to his or her demands, I advise my clients not to accept any telephone calls from the patient while in treatment. If necessary, an answering machine or Caller I.D. can be used to screen out the patient's calls. There is nothing to be gained from telephone calls, but there is a great deal to be lost if the patient manages to evade treatment by taking advantage of loved ones. The family is much better off keeping tabs on the patient's progress by staying in touch with the primary counselor.

Unfortunately, at many treatment centers, patients have easy access to both pay phones and personal cell phones. Still in the throes of illness, many alcoholics will call home incessantly, but families can take measures to prevent that from happening. Often the best course is for family members to arrange to speak to the alcoholic at most once or twice a week at a specified time when the patient can use a telephone under supervision in the counselor's office.

For the same reasons that I make every effort to minimize the number of telephone calls, I also discourage visiting by family members. I prefer to exclude visits altogether until the patient is ready to be discharged. Patients are usually not kept on locked wards, and they can walk out on their own. As such, whenever possible, the patient should not be allowed to enter treatment with credit cards or large sums of money, thus making it more difficult for the person to leave the center.

CASE NOTES: A TURNAROUND

In one instance, a young patient just left the treatment center shortly after being admitted. She sat on a corner with her suitcase for quite a while—about eight hours. She had no money and called her parents for help, but I persuaded them that to help her now would undermine any of the progress made. Finally, she called me and I convinced the treatment center to allow her back in and arranged for her to be picked up. This event became a complete turnaround for her. She finally believed that her parents had had enough. She has remained drug free after that traumatic time. If this young lady had money or a credit card, who knows how long it would have taken to get her back into treatment?

If a patient threatens to leave treatment early, the interventionist or counselor can step in, armed with the written statements used during the intervention. The counselor will remind the patient of that written testimony and the consequences that the alcoholic will suffer if he or she withdraws from treatment early. An alcoholic husband might be told, "You say you want to leave now, and you are free to go, but that would be a big mistake for you. Let me refresh your memory about what your family will do if you leave early. Your brother will no longer allow you in his home. Your children will no longer allow you to see your grandchildren. Your wife will leave you and file for divorce. You are going to blow this deal unless you stick with the program for another twenty-six days. Why not stay and put all of this behind you."

In my experience over the years, I have had very few patients leave early. Only rarely have I had to intervene a second time to convince the person to stay in treatment or to prolong the stay beyond 28 days. Depending on the patient's progress, counselors may advise extending the treatment time frame for one or more months. An important rule of thumb to keep in mind is that *the longer the treatment period is, the more likely the patient is to recover.* Some treatment centers require minimum stays of three to six months, and their success rates are often higher than short-term centers, reflecting the fact that extended inpatient care is more effective in bringing about full recovery.

WHAT TO EXPECT FROM TREATMENT PROGRAMS

Many people have unrealistic expectations about what treatment centers can actually deliver. Addiction is not like appendicitis—there is no quick, one-shot surgical procedure that remedies the disease once and for all. I think of clinical treatment as a form of intensive care—if the chemically dependent person doesn't get that care, he or she will succumb to the illness and become another fatality. Viewed in this way, treatment centers clearly provide invaluable, lifesaving services. But when people visit some high profile centers, they see magnificent country club and resort settings. The patients often have tans and may be swimming or jogging. That type of seemingly carefree scene affects the attitudes of outsiders and insurance companies, most of which will not cover extended care.

The luxurious, user-friendly environments of some treatment centers are designed to attract upscale patients, and the success rates of these centers are frequently reported as part of their marketing strategy. But without ongoing patient follow-up over a period of years, the numbers can be misleading. I tell each person who calls me that all of our efforts are aimed at getting the alcoholic into recovery, which means *fully recovered in the long run*. While intervention and clinical treatment are necessary starting points, they are only part of a much longer process. Many people fail to understand that the "long run" requires a lifelong commitment. They may think that after 28 days the patient will be "cured" or "fixed," and, unfortunately, that is almost never the case.

Sometimes a patient will be discharged from treatment and go home, and a family member will say, "I just spent all this money on you. You had your 28 days, and that's it." But 28 days is nothing more than a blink when you consider that many patients have been drinking or using with a single-minded focus for years. No one can address the problem adequately in such a short period of time, and that is one of the disturbing reasons many patients relapse. Some families think that treatment alone solves the problem. I call this the "appendectomy syndrome." Intervention and recovery are processes not events. Without a thoroughgoing plan for continuing care in conjunction with family counseling, most of them simply don't stand a chance after they return to the familiar temptations and social environment in which they were using in the past. This is one of the reasons that, in my practice, I continue to work with the patient regularly with a program of recovery management for at least a year after treatment.

Fortunately, many centers today offer a comprehensive, interdisciplinary approach to treatment, frequently involving a team of specialists that may include psychiatrists, psychologists, social counselors, chemical dependency counselors, physicians and nurses. But treatment facilities can vary a great deal in terms of their resources and quality of care. The best treatment programs stress long-term patient follow-up and aftercare. Some centers provide outpatient programs for two years or more, tracking the progress of patients through individual therapy sessions and family counseling. Sadly, there are some treatment centers that are seemingly more interested in keeping beds filled than providing quality care. Upon discharging the patient, the staff at such clinics may offer nothing more than an AA Big Book and wish the person good luck.

You will need to do some further research to be sure that the treatment center is equipped to meet your needs. I encourage my clients to visit the center whenever possible and meet with appropriate staff members before the patient is admitted. There are a number questions that you should ask, either in person or by phone, in order to find out about the type of care the patient will receive and what you can expect while the person is in treatment:

- Is the detoxification unit located within or outside the physical confines of the treatment facility? Keep in mind that when the detox unit is at a separate location like a hospital, there is a tendency after the 72-hour observation period for patients to attempt to go home rather than make the trip to the center to enter primary care.

- What contingency measures will be carried out by the staff in the event the patient tries to leave against medical advice? Some centers require the patient to make a formal written request for discharge with several days advance notice, and that allows time for the staff to dissuade the patient from trying to skip out on treatment.

- What kind of facilities and accommodations are provided in detox? Will the patient have a private room? How many physicians and nurses are on staff? Does the center provide a physical examination by a physician? Will the patient undergo a psychological evaluation by a psychiatrist? You will want to be assured the patient is going to be in qualified hands at all times while in detox and after being moved to the primary care unit.

- What happens if the patient should require medical care? Is the center affiliated with a hospital? How far is the nearest hospital? Will the center obtain medical records from the patient's personal physician, psychiatrist or therapist? Can the patient's stay in detox be extended if necessary? You will want to be sure that medical care is readily available 24 hours a day.

- Will the patient be assigned to a counselor after transferring to primary care? How often will the primary counselor meet with the patient? Two times a week? Five times? Is there a backup counselor who will be familiar with the patient's case and able to step in when the primary counselor is away? Whenever an issue arises for a patient in primary care, it is vitally important that the center have someone else on staff who will be up to speed on the patient's case and able to intervene effectively if necessary.

- How will the patient's time be spent in primary care? Are the patients kept active throughout the day? How much unsupervised downtime will the patient have? How often do patients attend group therapy? How may patients usually participate in a group therapy session? What is the age range of the patients in primary care?

- What is the patient's schedule on a typical day during primary care? What time is breakfast? Do patients make their own beds? What are the policies regarding televisions, computers and other electronic equipment? What supervised activities are scheduled on weekends?

- How many patients are assigned to a room? Can special diet needs be accommodated? Does the center offer a fitness or exercise program? What recreational activities does the center encourage? Is a patient likely to spend more time watching television than he or she spends in counseling or other supervised activities? Ideally, the patient should have a full schedule of supervised activities every day while in treatment. You will want to be assured that the program is intensive and that time is not being wasted.

- Does the center provide special services for patients with sight and hearing problems? Are attendants available to help older and disabled patients? Are there support groups to assist with special needs such as grief, legal or marital matters?

- What drugs are routinely administered to patients? In my practice, I avoid working with centers that prescribe tranquilizers or antidepressant medications to their patients. As I said before, alcoholism is the primary, underlying disease that needs to be addressed before other emotional disorders such as depression and anxiety can be properly diagnosed and treated. Even when tranquilizers and antidepressants are administered only in the short term, such medications serve to cushion the alcoholic from the negative consequences of drinking and using. However, if a patient enters treatment and is already addicted to a prescription drug such as Valium, the medical staff may have to implement a course of phased withdrawal in order to reduce the risk of seizures.

• Does the center offer Alcoholics Anonymous or other Twelve Step meetings? If so, how many meetings will the patient be required to attend during 28-day treatment period? Does the center provide family counseling programs?

• Does the center have an honor system that encourages patients to report anyone who brings alcohol or drugs into the center?

The staff at the center should be able to satisfy you with answers to such questions and should be held accountable for the quality of care provided. Remember that these centers operate as businesses, frequently charging $15,000 to $20,000 for their services. Many are staffed by devoted employees who give themselves daily to a difficult and often thankless job. Some centers are understaffed, with counselors assigned to a dozen or more patients and working under great duress. None of these institutions is perfect, but you have a right to demand a standard of care that can reasonably be expected to lead to recovery.

UNDERSTANDING THE ROLE OF ALCOHOLICS ANONYMOUS AND THE TWELVE STEP PROGRAM

Today most inpatient and outpatient programs in this country ally themselves with the Twelve Step groups such as Alcoholics Anonymous, Narcotics Anonymous, Al-Anon and Alateen. While based on the same twelve principles as AA, Al-Anon provides support for spouses and Alateen offers a similar program for the teenage children of alcoholics. You will be better able to understand the challenges that the alcoholic in your life now faces if you familiarize yourself to some extent with the basic principles of the Twelve Step program.

AA has been the target of criticism at various times during its first six decades, and the program may not be for everyone; but for the great majority of those alcoholics who attend meetings and commit themselves to the Twelve Step recovery process, AA serves as an effective support group and provides an essential lifeline to sobriety. There are other groups that offer alternative approaches to treating chemical dependency, but no other organization is as widely available as AA or as widely accepted within the mainstream medical community.

While the patient is in treatment, you would be wise to attend an open AA or NA meeting in your area to learn how the program is conducted. AA meetings can take various forms, but most are devoted to alcoholics discussing how drinking or using affected their lives and personalities, and what actions they have taken to address the problem. The organization describes itself as a fellowship and has always attempted to protect the anonymity of its members. Local Twelve Step meetings attract people from all walks of life, and the atmosphere and style of discourse can vary to some degree from group to group across the country. Some local groups may be more dynamic than others, some may seem more strict or doctrinaire in their approach, but the practical goals of each group and the Twelve Step strategy are the same everywhere.

These twelve principles are designed to address each facet of the alcoholic's life through a systematic process of mental and spiritual discipline. While there are explicit references to God and a "higher power," AA is not a religion. Even staunch atheists have been able to embrace the AA philosophy by adapting the program to fit their own needs and beliefs. I think of AA meetings simply as dress rehearsals for living a life of abstinence on a daily basis in the outside world. Exchanges with other alcoholics at the meetings reinforce the difficult lessons that the patient has learned in treatment. By working through the Twelve Steps over a period of months and years, the alcoholic learns to apply those lessons in life with the constant purpose of maintaining his or her sobriety.

The initial short-term period of clinical treatment will usually introduce the alcoholic to the basic concepts of the AA program. The first step involves an admission by the chemically dependent person that he or she is "powerless" to control his or her drinking or using. With the second step, the person defers to a "higher power" for relief and guidance. Some members think of the higher power concept as God, while others may think of it as the group itself. The first steps work on a premise that recovery from chemical dependency is not based on individual willpower but on a source of strength and conviction greater than one's self, whatever that might be for any individual.

In other words, AA requires the alcoholic to acknowledge the reality of the disease, and with that acknowledgment comes a recognition that recovery will entail an ongoing process of self-examination and personal growth. As the most accessible support group currently available, AA has come to play a key role in recovery management for millions of chemically dependent persons. But whether the recovering alcoholic joins AA or turns to private therapy or some other type of organized support, he or she needs to be prepared to make a lifelong commitment to abstinence. The bottom line is that after the patient is discharged from clinical treatment, that person is going to have to invest as much time and energy in recovery as he or she previously invested in the pursuit of alcohol and drugs. You will need to be ready to support that effort and to cope with changes in your own life that may accompany it.

CHAPTER SIX
SUMMARY POINTS

What happens in clinical treatment?

1. The patient will be admitted to a detox unit where he or she will be monitored for 48-72 hours or more.

2. After detox, the patient will be transferred to primary care to be educated about the disease and his or her condition.

3. Primary care includes lectures, counseling, group therapy and Twelve Step meetings.

4. Successful treatment should prepare the person to accept that he or she has a disease that only total abstinence can hold in check.

What can you expect from the patient during clinical treatment?

1. The patient may try to win your support for his or her early release.

2. The patient may attempt to contact you repeatedly and unnecessarily by telephone.

3. The patient may lie to you about the clinic and quality of care that he or she is receiving.

4. The patient may attack or blame you for getting him or her into treatment.

What should you expect from the treatment center?

1. The center should provide for detoxification either on site or at an outside facility.

2. The center should provide ongoing medical care with qualified professionals available at all times.

3. The center should provide for intensive primary care with close supervision of all patient activities.

4. The center should provide continuing care and follow-up after the patient is discharged from treatment

What should the alcoholic learn from treatment?

1. That alcoholism/drug addiction is a disease.

2. That the patient has the disease.

3. That the only way to treat the disease is total abstinence.

4. That the best way to maintain abstinence is through a 12-Step Program.

CHAPTER SEVEN

CONTINUING CARE AND LONG-TERM RECOVERY

What to Expect After Treatment

In my practice, when a patient is being discharged from treatment, I travel to the treatment center, either with or on behalf of my clients, to meet with the primary counselor and to transport the patient home. The counselor will give me and the patient's family or employer a full report on how the person has responded to treatment. If you are the one who meets with the counselor, you will want to obtain a detailed assessment of the patient's attitude and prognosis. Most importantly, on the basis of that assessment, the counselor or interventionist will provide a list of continuing care recommendations for the patient and family. The patient cannot be forced to comply with these recommendations, but he or she should understand their importance and agree to such a plan before returning home.

I advise patients to post the list of recommendations as a daily reminder on a refrigerator or bulletin board in the home. The continuing care plan may include outpatient counseling and daily consultations, in person or by phone, with the interventionist, therapist or some other professional for at least the first six to eight weeks after discharge. In some cases, these follow-up consultations may continue for a year or more. The patient will be asked to attend at least one AA or related Twelve Step meeting every day for the first three months after discharge. Whenever possible, the first meeting should take place on the same day that the patient returns home.

Arrangements can be made to have someone in the group welcome the patient to his or her first meeting. The alcoholic is embarking on a lifelong journey, and this first step needs to be undertaken immediately with the support of his or her family. *I encourage people to go to ninety meetings in ninety days. Give it a chance; it WILL happen to you. Even if you just show up. It's sometimes almost osmotic.*

The patient should also undergo a complete medical examination by a physician as soon as possible after being discharged from treatment. During the exam, the patient needs to make a full disclosure of his or her history of chemical dependency. It is important at this point for the patient to sit down with a doctor in confidence and be able to admit, "I'm an alcoholic, and I've just been released from treatment." Voicing those words indicates a fully conscious recognition of the illness and a willingness to confront the problem. Of course, there are patients who try to minimize their condition and waver in their resolve. Some patients will initially acquiesce and merely go through the motions of the recovery program. Yet even that minimal degree of commitment represents an acceptable beginning. Nothing is accomplished overnight, and the continuing care plan is designed to address that type of passive resistance from the outset.

Once a patient starts to attend AA meetings regularly, he or she will be encouraged to find a temporary "sponsor" in the group to help familiarize the person with the basics of the AA program. Newcomers are welcomed and receive enthusiastic moral support for their efforts. They are usually regarded as the most important people in the group and treated as such, because those who have been in the program for any length of time remember their own period of initiation into sobriety. A temporary sponsor can provide private counseling and assistance during moments of crisis as the patient adjusts to the day to day challenge of maintaining abstinence. Eventually, a permanent sponsor will work with the person on further understanding the AA philosophy and working through the Twelve Steps on a continuing basis. Each yearly anniversary in the program will be celebrated as a milestone of accomplishment.

Patients just out of treatment are sometimes reluctant to recruit sponsors for themselves. Although many addicts appear assertive and confident on the surface, they are often deeply afraid of rejection. Consequently, a patient may be apprehensive at first about approaching a stranger and asking for help. The newcomer to AA should be made aware that he or she might be turned down by a potential sponsor simply because that person may already be sponsoring several others and not be able to take on the additional responsibility. This is not the sort of rejection to be taken personally. Depending on the group, it may require several weeks or even months for the patient to find an appropriate sponsor and become acclimated to the routine of AA meetings.

I advise newcomers to get into the habit after meetings of writing down exactly what they liked, what they didn't like, and what they didn't understand. If a person repeatedly tells me that he or she liked everything and understood everything, then either that person is not actually going to the meetings or is still mentally disoriented, even though he or she may not be drinking or using. In order to encourage more active participation, I will suggest that the person approach the secretary of the group and volunteer to help set up for the meeting—stacking chairs, putting out literature, making coffee and so forth. The secretary is likely to ask the person to come early to the next meeting, thereby confirming a greater level of commitment.

The newcomer urgently needs to develop a social circle that supports abstinence, and AA is an arena where new friendships and healthy relationships can be established. I advise patients to devote at least fifteen minutes a day to reading AA literature and to actively participate in AA-sponsored social activities. Most Twelve Step groups promote picnics, softball games, dinners, outings to museums, and similar opportunities to socialize informally outside the structured group setting. While there may be a bad apple or two in any group, most recovering alcoholics are decent enough people who have every reason to help and support each other. Many recovering alcoholics establish lifelong friendships with others in the program.

After returning home from treatment, the patient needs to break off all relationships with past drinking and drug buddies. As difficult as this may be, those old ties must now be cut once and for all.

CASE NOTES: THE OLD GANG

One guy, a handsome, avant-garde, entertainment industry type, spent a lot of time with a particular group of guys drinking, carousing, etc. When he returned from treatment, he was eager to show off how he could do the same thing but drink only spring water. After an evening or two with his old buddies, he realized that the outing was boring and, in fact, wondered how he ever stood these people.

Sometimes the physical environment in the home will have to be changed if the alcoholic associates a particular room or ambience with past abuse. The person may have had a favorite chair or table where he or she was in the habit of drinking or using. Such furnishings should be removed before the patient comes home from treatment. Every possible measure of this kind needs to be taken in advance to facilitate the transition to a clean and sober lifestyle.

GUARDING AGAINST RELAPSE

If someone suggests to a recovering alcoholic, "Oh, come on, one glass of wine won't hurt you," that person is unwittingly encouraging a relapse and needs to be set straight in no uncertain terms. Your vigilant support and that of your intervention team can be crucial in this regard. By taking part in the person's recovery program—by going to AA and Al-Anon meetings, by communicating and monitoring progress on a daily basis—you can make an invaluable contribution to the patient's long-term recovery. The family's active involvement in the continuing care program can effectively rule out the possibility of relapse.

The initial phase of adjustment after treatment is a transitional rite of passage that can be agonizing for patients. The first year is usually the greatest challenge, and many alcoholics experience this period as a kind of penance. The person is likely to be carrying a great deal of emotional baggage left over from his or her days of drinking or using: resentments, fear of failure, feelings of inadequacy, fear of intimacy, a need to control others, isolation, anxiety, depression, and so forth. During the first months of abstinence, the anguish that was previously dulled by alcohol or drugs can rise to the surface. I was told early in my recovery that sometimes there would be nothing to do other than to sit in pain and not drink. But over time in most cases, those difficult moments and the temptation to return to drinking or using become less and less frequent, eventually ceasing altogether.

Alcoholics in recovery can always find a reason to drink or use, but relapses are not inevitable. While many professionals in the field acknowledge that some patients initially fail to adjust to the demands of abstinence and require more than one course of clinical treatment, relapses should not be viewed as a normal or necessary part of the recovery process. I frequently get calls from patients who painfully confess, "I just feel like having a drink." Such cravings are natural, and each crisis of this sort needs to be handled through ongoing counseling and group interactions. Many sponsors make themselves available day and night to offer round the clock assistance as the patient develops daily coping skills.

One of the best tools for recovery is a good memory. The alcoholic will remember the humiliation of being in handcuffs, or waking up with a black eye, or the shame of being fired from his or her job. We all have those memories, like scenes from a movie that we never want to live through again. I may tell a vacillating patient, "You don't want to go back to that nightmare again. Just stick it out for another few hours and get through this stretch until you can make it to your next meeting." This type of hand-holding is crucial, whether provided by a sponsor, a therapist or by someone else who cares for the person and knows the addict's mentality.

Relapses in my practice are rare, but they can occur early in recovery if a patient fails to take the first steps to consciously recognize the disease, or later in recovery, if the patient becomes complacent and falsely assumes that he or she can return to moderate use. When a relapse does occur, there is no alternative but to intervene again. An intervention may be more difficult the second time around because the alcoholic knows what to expect. Nevertheless, even under the most adverse circumstances, effective leverage can once again be brought to bear on the alcoholic, who is likely to be feeling remorse and shame after the transgression. A relapse gives the interventionist and the family additional, irrefutable proof of the reality of the problem and strengthens the case for long-term clinical treatment as the most viable recourse for the patient.

FAMILY RECOVERY

I caution family members that after treatment they are going to get back a different person than the one they knew before. The early stages of abstinence are often marked by profound personality changes, and, therefore, family members need to be prepared to face challenges and to make adjustments in their personal lives. I strongly advise the family not to dwell on the alcoholic's past behavioral lapses. Those issues will be addressed and amends will be made through the AA program.

Professional care for the entire family is essential in many cases. Where a wife may have been paying the bills and running the household while her husband was in treatment, he may want to take control again after returning home. Yet his wife may not want to relinquish the purse strings. She may not trust his newfound commitment to abstinence, and when she voices her fears, the husband may interpret her concern as an attack. In order to resolve such marital disputes, they will both need counseling to learn how to actively participate in recovery together.

I often hear the non-drinking wife say, "But he's the sick one, why do I have to do anything?" Or the non-drinking husband may complain, "She's the one with the alcohol problem, why can't I have my two scotches before dinner anymore? Why do I have to give that up?" The answers to such questions should be a matter of common sense, but there is sometimes very little of that to go around. The husband may expect his wife to go to ninety AA meetings in ninety days while he refuses to attend even a single meeting with her. With husbands and wives, if one or the other comes out of treatment and the spouse fails to participate in the recovery program, I can almost guarantee that the marriage will be dead or in serious trouble within two years.

A legendary CEO of a treatment center, now deceased, warned me, "Bruce, in six minutes, the family can reverse the work we did in six months." I've seen that kind of scenario played out any number of times. Both spouses can become very stubborn and self-righteous. The husband or the wife may be a drinker, a pot smoker, or a cocaine user, and he or she comes back from treatment committed to abstinence. Now that person starts going to AA meetings faithfully and not using. The non-participating spouse often becomes jealous of the relationships that the alcoholic develops through the meetings. But for recovering patients, those meetings are the life-or-death equivalent to renal dialysis. With the zeal of the converted, they will go to meetings even if they have to travel through a blizzard and miss a family gathering.

Even under the best circumstances, the non-drinking spouse is likely to resent the time the husband or wife is spending away from the family. The husband may get home from work at six o'clock, and by seven o'clock he is on his way out the door to another meeting. The wife will call me and ask, "How long does he have to go to these meetings?"—as if the person were going to graduate at some point. It is sometimes said that the only thing worse than being an alcoholic is being married to one. This might also apply to a recovering alcoholic, but it doesn't have to be that way if both spouses make a sincere commitment from the outset to become involved in the program together.

When jointly undertaken, the process of recovery can strengthen a marriage and benefit both partners. Sobriety doesn't have to be a bleak undertaking—it can and should be a shared joy, a life-affirming adventure that opens new horizons. In my case, except for the anguish and hurt that I caused others while I was drinking, I wouldn't have missed the experience of recovery for anything in the world.

Recently, one of my clients, a woman whose husband was about to go into treatment, confronted me with her misgivings. She said, "You've been sober for years. But is your life really different? Was it worth it?" I was amazed when I realized that she was actually suggesting that it might be better for her husband not to deal with his problem. I told her, "Everything in my life has changed. I'm a loving husband now, and I'm a good father. When I say that I'm going to be home at seven, I am home at seven. The bills are paid, and our lives have been enriched. We communicate with honesty, and we look forward to each day together and face whatever challenges come our way. When I was in treatment, I remember being told that if I made the effort, eventually every morning would be like Christmas, filled with unexpected joy, and that is exactly what happened. My recovery has led to more blessings than my wife and I ever could have imagined, and there is no reason that it can't be the same for you."

My life is continually filled with this joy, especially my family life. Our son Quinn is in the third grade, and recently his teacher asked the class to write about an important person. His teacher showed me what he wrote:

My character is my father, Bruce Cotter. He looks handsome and athletic. Also he looks smart. His job is being an interventionist. That means he talks to people about drinking. Of course, his biggest job is being my Dad. Sometimes he coaches my sports teams. Some feelings that I have for him are that I like to be with him. I have always been proud to say he is honest. He says to me When you are not practicing somewhere some guy is. And when you meet, he will win. I take his advice.

You can imagine how I felt when I read it. This would not have been written without my sobriety.

I continue to regard my sobriety as nothing less than a rebirth—a thoroughgoing change of consciousness that has instilled meaning and purpose in my life. Thanks to treatment and the steadfast support of my wife, I was given a second chance. My personal experience is not unique but shared by countless others who have managed to recover their lives, some of whom I have been fortunate enough to assist by pointing the way toward intervention and treatment. If I have been able to provide you with a practical sense of direction and a measure of hope as you now try to help the chemically dependent person in your life, then you have afforded me with the opportunity to give something back to those whose love and care sustained me. Though our paths may never cross, may your efforts be as richly rewarded as mine have been.

CHAPTER SEVEN
SUMMARY POINTS

Continuing care recommendations for
the patient after treatment:

1. Total abstinence from alcohol and drugs.

2. Daily contact by phone or in person with the interventionist, counselor and/or therapist.

3. A medical examination with full disclosure of the addiction and treatment history.

4. Select a temporary "home group" for Twelve Step meetings.

5. Attend at least one Twelve Step (AA) meeting every day for ninety days.

6. Participate verbally at every Twelve Step meeting and thank the speaker afterwards.

7. Volunteer to be of service at Twelve Step meetings (set up, make coffee, etc.).

8. Write down what you liked, didn't like and didn't understand after each meeting.

9. Read Twelve Step literature at least fifteen minutes each day.

10. Recruit a Twelve Step sponsor.

11. Participate in Twelve Step sponsored social activities (outings, dinners, etc.).

12. Start to cultivate friendships in the Twelve Step group and encourage family participation.

WHERE TO GET HELP
TREATMENT CENTERS

Caron Foundation
(Adolescent and Adult Treatment Facility)
Box 150
Galen Hall Road
Wernersville, PA 19565
Telephone: (800) 678-2332
Website: www.caron.org

Colonial House
(Adult Treatment Facility)
1300 Woodbury Road
York, PA 17404
Telephone: (717) 792-9702
FAX: (717) 792-9910
Website: www.colonialhouseinc.com
E-mail: admissions@colonialhouse.org

Hanley-Hazelden
(Adult and Older Adult Treatment Facility)
5200 East Avenue
West Palm Beach, FL 33407
Telephone: (800) 444-7008
              (561) 841-1000
FAX: (561) 841-1100
Website: www.hazelden.org

Little Hill - Alina Lodge
(Long Term - Adult Treatment Facility)
Box G
Blairstown, NJ 07825
Telephone: (800) 57-LODGE (575-6343)
              (908) 363-6114
Website: www.alinalodge.org
e-mail: jackim@alinalodge.org

149

SUPPORT GROUPS

Alcoholics Anonymous
World Service
Grand Central Station
P.O. Box 459
New York, NY 10163
Telephone (212) 870-3400
Website: www.alcoholicsanonymous.org

Narcotics Anonymous
World Service
P.O. Box 9999
Van Nuys, CA 91409
Telephone: (818) 773-9999
FAX: (818) 700-0700
Website: www.na.org
E-mail: fsmail@na.org

Alanon and Alateen
World Service
1600 Corporate Landing Parkway
Virginia Beach, VA 23454-5617
Telephone: (757) 563-1600
Worldwide Meeting Information: (888) 425-2666
Website: www.al-anon.alateen.org
E-mail: wso@al-anon.org

NATIONAL & GOVERNMENT AGENCIES

The Substance Abuse and Mental Health
  Services Administration
Office of Communications: (301) 443-8956
Toll free: (800) 662-HELP
E-mail: info@samhsa.gov
Website: www.samhsa.gov/

National Institute of Alcohol Abuse and Alcoholism
(NIAAA)
Department of Health and Human Services
Telephone: (301) 443-3885
Website: www.niaaa.nih.gov/

Employee Assistance Professionals Association (EAP)
Telephone: (703) 387-1000
Website: www.eap-association.com

NOTES

ABOUT THE AUTHOR

Bruce Cotter is the senior partner of Bruce Cotter and Associates, a national Intervention and Recovery Management firm. He excelled at many things in life-education, competitive sports, and a career in broadcasting until alcoholism cost him all he loved and achieved. Today, Cotter has earned the reputation as America's leading interventionist. Cotter is the one the CEOs of major corporations, national government agencies and senior staff members of treatment centers call when they have a personal interest in an individual with a chemical dependency problem. Trained at the Johnson Institute, under Reverend Vernon Johnson, in St. Paul, the Employee Assistance Program at Loyola College in Baltimore, and mainly, at the "school of hard knocks," Cotter brings a fierce and competitive resolve to his work. Cotter was born and educated in Philadelphia. He is an avid fisherman and enjoys coaching his son's baseball and basketball teams. With offices in Baltimore and Palm Beach, Florida, Cotter resides with his wife and son in the Maryland countryside.